Weight Watchers

The SmartPoints Diet Plan - Delicious Recipes For Rapid Weight Loss

JOANNA SMITH

Copyright © 2016 Joanna Smith

All rights reserved.

© **Copyright 2016 - All rights reserved.**

In no way is it legal to reproduce, duplicate, or transmit any part of this document in either electronic means or in printed format. Recording of this publication is strictly prohibited and any storage of this document is not allowed unless with written permission from the publisher. All rights reserved.

The information provided herein is stated to be truthful and consistent, in that any liability, in terms of inattention or otherwise, by any usage or abuse of any policies, processes, or directions contained within is the solitary and utter responsibility of the recipient reader. Under no circumstances will any legal responsibility or blame be held against the publisher for any reparation, damages, or monetary loss due to the information herein, either directly or indirectly.
Respective authors own all copyrights not held by the publisher.

Legal Notice:
This book is copyright protected. This is only for personal use. You cannot amend, distribute, sell, use, quote or paraphrase any part or the content within this book without the consent of the author or copyright owner. Legal action will be pursued if this is breached.

Disclaimer Notice:

Please note the information contained within this document is for educational and entertainment purposes only. Every attempt has been made to provide accurate, up to date and reliable complete information. No warranties of any kind are expressed or implied. Readers acknowledge that the author is not engaging in the rendering of legal, financial, medical or professional advice.

By reading this document, the reader agrees that under no circumstances are we responsible for any losses, direct or indirect,
which are incurred as a result of the use of information contained within this document, including, but not limited to, —errors, omissions, or inaccuracies.

Table of Contents

Introduction

Chapter 1: Breakfast

Chapter 2: Main Dishes

Chapter 3: Desserts

Chapter 4: Snacks And Appetizers

Chapter 5: Drinks

Chapter 6: Vegetarians And Weight Watchers

Chapter 7: Vegans And Weight Watchers

Chapter 8: Weight Watchers At Christmas

Chapter 9: Weight Watchers And Exercise

Chapter 10: Tips For Increasing Water Consumption Every Day

Chapter 11: Cheat Days? Yes Or No

Chapter 12: Who Can Do Weight Watchers

Chapter 13: Success Stories

Chapter 14: Tips For Success From The Successful

Chapter 15: Interesting Facts About Weight Watchers

Conclusion

Introduction

This book will provide you with an extensive variety of recipes that are designed to work with Weight Watchers' new points system, SmartPoints. Each recipe has a specific SmartPoints value set out, and they will all allow you to keep to your SmartPoints budget. On top of being healthy and working with your Weight Watchers plan, the recipes are also amazingly delicious and fun. Even your family, friends, and guests will love them too!

The SmartPoints system provides a points value for various foods. The points are assessed based on four components: saturated fat, sugar, protein, and calories. A higher points value means that a certain food is 'unhealthier' overall; lean protein reduces the points value while saturated fat and sugar would increase the points value.

Your SmartPoints 'budget' is calculated based on your height, gender, current weight, and age, and gives a daily allowance and a weekly allowance. The weekly allowance is for the purpose of fitting in 'splurges', such as a special dessert or a night out with friends.

The overall theme of the SmartPoints system is that no food or drink is 'off the menu', so to speak. You can eat any variation of food that you want, but you have to make sure that you are eating within your SmartPoints budget. This encourages healthier and more nutritious eating, without forcing you to give up flavor and meal selections.

When you are determining the SmartPoints value of a recipe, it is important to remember that certain foods (mostly veggies and fruits) are assigned a points value of zero. So for example, a chicken pasta dish will include the points value for the sauce, the pasta, and the chicken, but not for any veggies that are added to the sauce or on top of the pasta.

Many of the recipes that are in this book are vegetarian or vegan, or can be easily made vegetarian or vegan. Just remember that if you are substituting items into recipes for any reason, you will need to do your own calculations of the SmartPoints value in order to ensure that you are still properly keeping track of your daily and weekly points allowances.

The SmartPoints system is a convenient and less restrictive diet than most, and it will allow you to lose weight, but at a healthy pace while still enjoying the foods you love. I hope that you will enjoy the recipes that I have included with this book and that you will find them helpful when it comes to working within your SmartPoints budget. I wish you the best of luck with your Weight Watchers plan.

Chapter 1: Breakfast

Starting your day with a nutritious and balanced meal is the best way to make sure that you have the energy and ability required to get you through your day. The recipes set out in this chapter will help provide you with that necessary (and delicious) start to the day.

Breakfast is the most important meal of the day. Eating a decent breakfast will help your metabolism kick into gear for the entire day. Try to change up your breakfast and make minor adjustments to old recipes to make it interesting.

Breakfast Hash

Have some leftover ingredients in the fridge? With just an egg and a few vegetables, you can create a seemingly minute amount of food into full blown breakfast recipe. This recipe gives you a feisty southern taste with the comfort of breakfast aromas sizzling from the frying pan.

Preparation time: 15 minutes

Cook time: 10 minutes

INGREDIENTS

Non-stick cooking spray

1 cup of frozen, shredded potatoes or (you could also grate your own)

1-2 slices of chopped sweet onion

1 tbsp. (7g) real bacon bits

1 slice of Canadian bacon cubed

1/3 of a chopped red bell pepper

1 handful of baby spinach leaves chopped

1 egg beaten

DIRECTIONS

Spray skillet with nonstick spray and place over medium heat. Add the frozen potatoes. Leave them alone for approximately 5 minutes while you chop all the other ingredients. Flip the potatoes. This will thaw and begin to brown the potatoes.

Once you notice that they are starting to brown, cook them for another 3 or 4 minutes. Add in the onion and bacon bits. Since we are not using oil, the potatoes will not brown like traditional hash browns usually do.

Once the onion and bacon bits are added, continue to cook over medium heat until the onion softens. Add the Canadian bacon and bell pepper. Cook for a few minutes allowing the flavors to merge.

Add the chopped spinach and stir in. As soon as it starts to wilt, pour in the beaten egg. Immediately start to combine and mix in the egg. After the egg coats everything in the pan, use your spatula to press the hash down. It will create a nice brown on the bottom and "stick" the hash together a bit. Leave it alone for a minute.

Flip the skillet onto a plate and serve with some ketchup!

Makes 1 serving

NUTRITIONAL VALUE

1 breakfast hash: 242 calories, 8g fat (3g saturated fat), 5g fiber, 5g sugar, 16g carbs, 20g protein

SmartPoint Value: 5

Banana Bread

While this recipe may not look like a healthy option at first, it is quite reasonable compared to a lot of banana bread recipes, thanks especially to the use of egg whites instead of whole eggs, and the I Can't Believe It's Not Butter! ® This recipe lets you feel like you are cheating, while still easily fitting into your daily allowance.

Preparation time: 10 minutes

Cook time: 55 minutes

INGREDIENTS

1 ½ cups whole-wheat flour

½ cup brown sugar (loose, do not pack)

2 tsp. baking powder

½ tsp. salt

1 ½ tsp. cinnamon

½ cup egg whites

1 ½ cups (approx. 3 large) extra-ripe mashed bananas

¾ cup I Can't Believe It's Not Butter! ® Original Spread

1 tsp. vanilla extract

DIRECTIONS

Preheat the oven to 350 degrees Fahrenheit. Using non-stick spray, spray a 9" x 13" loaf pan.

Combine flour, sugar, salt, ½ tsp. of cinnamon, and baking powder in a large bowl, and mix thoroughly.

Combine the egg whites, bananas, vanilla extract, and ½ cup of the I Can't Believe It's Not Butter! ®. Whisk these ingredients until uniform.

Combine the wet ingredients with the dry ingredients, and mix them until they are uniform.

Place the batter into the loaf pan, smoothing out the surface.

Bake the bread for approximately 50 minutes, until a toothpick can be inserted into the center of the loaf, and comes out clean.

Once finished, cut the loaf into twelve slices. When you are ready to eat, toast each slice and then butter it with one teaspoon of the remaining I Can't Believe It's Not Butter! ® and a sprinkle of the remaining 1 tsp. of cinnamon.

Makes 12 servings.

NUTRITIONAL VALUE

Per 1 slice (1/12th of the recipe): 169 calories, 287mg sodium, 6.5g total fat (2g sat fat), 24g carbs, 9.5g sugars, 2.5g fiber, 3.5g protein

SmartPoints Value: 5

Crust-less Quiche

What breakfast is complete without quiche? This recipe adds the aromatic flavors of garlic and onion while keeping the flavor mild and delicious. The addition of egg whites and broccoli makes this delectable dish yummy and healthy.

Preparation time: 15 minutes

Cooking time: 35 minutes

INGREDIENTS

1 cup liquid egg whites

1/2 cup of reduced-fat 2% milk

1 cup of cooked and chopped broccoli florets

1/2 cup chopped cherry tomatoes

3/4 cup reduced-fat sharp cheddar shredded cheese

1 tsp. of garlic powder

1 tsp. of onion powder

1/4 tsp. of paprika

Salt and pepper to taste

DIRECTIONS

Preheat oven to 350. Spray four 8oz ramekins with nonfat butter flavored cooking spray. Place ramekins on baking sheet.

In a medium sized bowl, whisk all of the ingredients together; egg whites, milk, paprika, garlic powder, onion powder, salt, and pepper. Finally, stir in the cheese, tomatoes and broccoli.

Using a spoon, scoop the egg mixture evenly into each ramekin. Try and make sure there is an even amount into each prepared ramekin, and bake 30-

35 minutes, until the egg is thoroughly cooked, and a light golden brown.

Makes 4 servings.

NUTRITIONAL VALUE

1 quiche (serving): 125 calories, 5g fat, 11g protein, 4g carbs, 1g fiber

SmartPoints Value: 3

Individual Ham and Cheese Frittata's

Frittata is one arguably one of the most versatile breakfast dishes. With the ability to add almost any ingredient, a frittata can take on the flavor of almost an ingredient you add to it while also being healthy and nutritional.

Preparation time: 15 minutes

Cook time: 25 minutes

INGREDIENTS

Cooking spray

1 pound frozen hash brown potatoes, thawed

4 large eggs, beaten

1 tbsp. fat-free milk

Salt and pepper to taste

2-oz cooked lean ham, finely chopped

2 tbsp. finely chopped sweet red bell pepper

2 tbsp. finely chopped green bell pepper

2 tbsp. finely chopped onion

½ cup low-fat shredded cheddar cheese

DIRECTIONS

Defrost the hash browns by leaving them on the counter away from heat.

Position an oven rack in the center of your oven and preheat oven to 350 degrees Fahrenheit. Spray 8 muffin cups with cooking spray.

Firmly press the thawed potatoes into the bottom and along the sides of the muffin cups to form a crust.

Bake for 15 to 20 minutes.

Meanwhile, begin to make the filling: In a medium bowl beat the eggs and milk together, and season with salt and pepper. Stir in onion, ham, pepper and cheese until blended.

Remove potatoes from the oven and press them firmly with a spoon so that they are similar to mini pie crusts, lining the bottom and sides of each of the muffin cups.

Divide the mixture evenly, pouring it into each of the muffin cups.

Return to the oven and bake until potatoes are crisp and golden brown, and the egg mixture is set, for 15 to 18 minutes.

Remove from the oven and let sit for around 5 minutes before serving.

Makes 8 servings.

NUTRITIONAL VALUE

1 serving (1 frittata): Nutritional info N.A

SmartPointsValue: 3

French Toast Casserole

French toast is easy to cook and allows for the addition of different toppings including syrups, fruits, and spices. Another fantastic feature of French toast is the ability to make it into a casserole, as done in this recipe.

Preparation time: 10 minutes

Cook time: 1 hour

INGREDIENTS

5 cups bread cubes

4 eggs

1 1/2 cups milk

1/4 cup white sugar, divided

1/4 tsp. salt

1 tsp. vanilla extract

1 tbsp. softened margarine

1 tsp. ground cinnamon

DIRECTIONS

Preheat oven to 350 degrees Fahrenheit. Lightly butter an 8x8 inch baking pan.

Line the bottom of your pan with bread cubes. In a large, separate bowl, beat together eggs, milk, 2 tablespoons of sugar, salt and vanilla. Pour the egg mixture over the bread. Dot lightly with margarine and let it stand for 10 minutes.

Combine the remaining 2 tablespoons of sugar with 1 teaspoon of cinnamon and sprinkle over the top. Bake in a preheated oven for about 45 to 50 minutes, until the top, is golden and firm to the touch.

Makes 6 servings.

NUTRITIONAL VALUE

1 serving: 207 calories, 7g fat, 26g carbs, 1g fiber, 8.5g protein

SmartPoints Value: 5

Swiss Avocado Egg Mug

This recipe is a delicious and healthy option and is fast and easy to make. The spinach, mushrooms, and tomatoes provide a great serving of veggies while the egg substitute and low-fat cheese ensures that you are getting sufficient protein. The avocado is an excellent source of heart-healthy fat – and it's very tasty! Since you're only using a mug and a fork, this is also an easy prep and easy cleanup recipe.

Preparation time: 5 minutes

Cook time: 5 minutes

INGREDIENTS

½ cup sliced mushrooms

½ cup chopped fresh spinach

½ cup fat-free liquid egg substitute

1 wedge of The Laughing Cow Light Creamy Swiss cheese

2 tbsp. diced tomatoes

2 tbsp. (1 oz.) diced avocado

DIRECTIONS

Spray a large, microwave-safe mug with non-stick spray, and microwave the spinach and mushrooms for 1.5 minutes, or until soft.

Blot the excess moisture with paper towels, add the egg substitute, and stir. Microwave for 1 minute.

Mix the cheese and tomato into the mug, breaking the cheese into pieces to help it melt. Microwave for 1 minute, or until the dish sets. Top the mug with avocado and enjoy.

Makes 1 serving.

NUTRITIONAL VALUE

Per serving: 140 calories, 456mg sodium, 4.5g total fat (1.5g sat fat), 7g carbs, 3g sugars, 2g fiber, 16g protein

SmartPoints Value: 3

Classic Breakfast Sandwich

This recipe is a healthy, low-fat twist on a classic, and is incredibly easy to make. You can add veggies as toppings (avocado, tomatoes or mushrooms would be a fantastic addition) without adding to the SmartPoints value. If you enjoy ketchup on your breakfast toppings, you can add that without impacting the SmartPoints value.

Preparation time: 5 minutes

Cook time: 5 minutes

INGREDIENTS

½ cup fat-free liquid egg substitute

Dash each of salt and black pepper

Flat sandwich bun, ~100 calories

Slice of reduced-fat cheddar cheese

DIRECTIONS

Using non-stick spray, spray a medium-sized microwave-safe bowl. To assist, the bottom of the bowl should be approximately the size of the bun that you are using for the sandwich. Add the egg substitute, salt, and pepper to the bowl and microwave for 1 minute.

Stir gently, and microwave for another minute.

Put ½ of the bun on a microwave-safe plate, and top with the egg patty then the cheese. Then place the other ½ bun on top.

Microwave the sandwich for 20 seconds, or until the cheese is melted. Enjoy!

Makes 1 serving.

NUTRITIONAL VALUE

Per serving: 223 calories, 773mg sodium, 5.5g total fat (3g sat fat), 24g carbs, 3.5g sugars, 5g fiber, 22.5g protein

SmartPoints Value: 6

Southwestern Oven-Baked Omelet

While this recipe does take longer to make than most of the other recipes in this section, the final product is well worth the wait. Save it for a lazy weekend morning when you have time to spend both cooking and savoring this yummy dish. It can also easily be made vegan, although that will change the SmartPoints value so you will have to do your own calculations if you make substitutions.

Preparation time: 15 minutes

Cook time: 1 hour

INGREDIENTS

½ cup fat-free milk

2 ½ cups fat-free liquid egg substitute

½ tsp. taco seasoning mix

1 tsp. cumin

1 tsp. chopped garlic

½ cup chopped onion

½ cup chopped red bell pepper

½ cup canned sweet corn, drained

¼ cup canned, diced green chiles

½ cup canned black beans, drained and rinsed

Optional toppings: fat-free sour cream, salsa, chopped scallions

DIRECTIONS

Preheat the oven to 375 degrees Fahrenheit.

Take a deep 8" x 10" baking pan, and line it with aluminum foil. Using non-stick spray, lightly spray the sides and bottom of the pan.

Combine the milk, egg substitute, taco seasoning, and cumin in a large bowl, and whisk thoroughly.

Add garlic, onion, and bell pepper to the bowl. Stir well. Transfer the egg mixture from the bowl to the baking pan.

Add the corn, black beans, and green chiles to the pan evenly, and sprinkle the dish with cheese.

Bake until the center of the omelet is firm, and the top is puffed. Approximately 1 hour.

Allow the omelet to cool, and divide into four servings. Add optional toppings if desired.

Makes 4 servings.

NUTRITIONAL VALUE

¼ of the recipe: 188 calories, 590mg sodium, 3g total fat (1.5g sat fat), 17g carbs, 5g sugars, 2.5g fiber, 22g protein

SmartPoints Value: 4

<u>Fruit-tastic Quinoa Bowl</u>

This recipe is a berry lover's dream, and it is also completely vegan. Quinoa is a wonderful alternative to the more traditional oatmeal, as it is very high in fiber, protein, and an assortment of vitamins. It is also an excellent option for anyone who is required to eat a gluten-free diet.

Preparation time: 5 minutes

Cook time: 15 minutes

INGREDIENTS

¼ cup uncooked quinoa rinsed thoroughly

1/8 tsp. cinnamon

1 no-calorie sweetener packet

Dash of salt

1/3 cup water

¾ cup Unsweetened Vanilla Almond Breeze (almond milk)

¼ cup raspberries

¼ cup blueberries

¼ cup chopped strawberries

DIRECTIONS

Using a non-stick pot, combine the quinoa, cinnamon, sweetener, and salt. Mix in the water and Almond Breeze.

Bring to a boil, and then reduce the heat to a simmer. Cook 12-14 minutes until most of the liquid has been absorbed, and the quinoa is fully cooked, stirring frequently.

Mix the berries in, and transfer to a bowl.

Makes 1 serving.

NUTRITIONAL VALUE

1 serving: 252 calories, 295mg sodium, 5.5g total fat (0g sat fat), 45.5g carbs, 8g sugars, 8g fiber, 7.5g protein

SmartPoints Value: 6

Eggs and Bacon Waffle Taco

Nothing about this recipe sounds like it could possibly be a healthy option that would fit into your SmartPoints budget, but it actually is a great breakfast option. The fat-free egg substitute and low-fat cheese used helps to reduce the calorie and fat content, lowering the points value while still providing plenty of protein. Eating this dish feels naughty, but it's actually very nice!

Preparation time: 5 minutes

Cook time: 15 minutes

Cooling time: 10 minutes

INGREDIENTS

1 frozen, low-fat waffle, thawed

1/3 cup fat-free liquid egg substitute

1 tbsp. precooked real crumbled bacon

2 tbsp. shredded reduced-fat cheddar cheese

Optional topping: sugar-free pancake syrup

DIRECTIONS

Preheat the oven to 425 degrees Fahrenheit.

Place the thawed waffle on a flat, dry surface. Flatten it as much as possible, using a rolling pin. Drape the waffle evenly over the side of a 9" x 5" loaf pan, so that it looks like an upside-down taco.

Bake the waffle for about 10 minutes until it is crispy and firm.

Remove the waffle from the pan and let it cool completely or for about 10 minutes.

Using non-stick spray, spray a microwave-safe mug. Microwave the egg substitute for 1minute, or until set. Stir the bacon and cheese into the mug, or you can sprinkle them over the taco after it's assembled with the egg.

Put the egg scramble into the taco.

Makes 1 serving.

NUTRITIONAL VALUE

1 serving: 190 calories, 636mg sodium, 6g total fat (3g sat fat), 16.5g carbs, 2g sugars, 2g fiber, 17g protein

SmartPoints Value: 5

Pancakes Galore

Pancakes are another classic breakfast item, and it is always useful to have a recipe available that will allow you to enjoy this tradition while sticking to your SmartPoints budget. The SmartPoints value for this recipe does not include toppings, but there are many toppings that will add little to no points: fruit is an excellent example, as is sugar-free syrup. Adjust your SmartPoints accordingly if you choose items like chocolate chips or peanut butter to satisfy your sweet tooth.

Preparation time: 5 minutes

Cook time: 10 minutes

INGREDIENTS

1/3 cup whole-wheat flour

1 no-calorie sweetener packet

½ tsp. baking powder

¼ cup fat-free liquid egg substitute

¼ cup water

1/8 tsp. vanilla extract

Optional seasonings: salt, cinnamon

DIRECTIONS

Mix the flour, sweetener, baking powder, and salt (if using) in a medium bowl. Stir in the egg substitute, water, and vanilla extract.

Spray a skillet with non-stick spray, and bring it to medium-high heat. Form a large pancake with half of the batter. Cook the pancake until it is starts to bubble and is solid enough to be flipped, 2-3 minutes. Flip the pancake and cook it until both sides are lightly browned, and the inside is cooked, 1-2 minutes.

Repeat using the remaining batter to make the second pancake.

Makes 1 serving.

NUTRITIONAL VALUE

1 serving (2 pancakes): 180 calories, 515mg sodium, 1g total fat (0g sat fat), 32g carbs, 1g sugars, 5g fiber, 11.5g protein

SmartPoints Value: 4

Apple Cinnamon Breakfast Bowl

This recipe is one that is incredibly easy and quick to make, and the finished product is not only delicious but also provides a great serving of protein and fiber. With a SmartPoints value of only two per serving, this breakfast bowl would make an excellent start to the day.

Preparation time: 5 minutes

INGREDIENTS

½ cup fat-free cottage cheese

1 drop vanilla extract

½ tsp. cinnamon divided evenly in half

1 no-calorie sweetener packet

1 Fuji apple, cored and cubed

DIRECTIONS

Combine the cottage cheese, vanilla extract, cinnamon, and sweetener into a bowl, and mix well.

Top the bowl with the apple cubes, sprinkle with the remaining cinnamon.

Makes 1 serving.

NUTRITIONAL VALUE

1 serving: 182 calories, 429mg sodium, 0.5g total fat (0g sat fat), 32.5g carbs, 5g 24g sugars, fiber, 13.5g protein

SmartPoints Value: 4

Double Chocolate Bran Muffins

Packed with fiber and chocolate, these muffins offer benefits to your cardiovascular and gastrointestinal health. On top of health benefits, these muffins are full of chocolatey goodness that will keep you coming back for more – which in this case, isn't a bad thing.

Preparation time: 15 minutes

Cook time: 20 minutes

INGREDIENTS

1 cup of Fiber One Cereal, crush after measuring

1⅓ cups of buttermilk or 1¼ cup regular milk plus 4 tsps. of vinegar

¼ cup canola oil

1 large egg

¾ cup packed brown sugar

1 tsp. vanilla

½ cup unsweetened baking cocoa

1 tsp. baking soda

¼ tsp. salt

1 cup white whole wheat flour

⅓ cup mini semi-sweet chocolate chips

DIRECTIONS

Preheat the oven to 375 degrees Fahrenheit and line 10 muffin cups with paper liners.

Crush the Fiber One Cereal in a Ziploc bag with a rolling pin; you can also crush using your fists or a meat tenderizer.

In a mixing bowl, combine crushed cereal with the buttermilk. Let mixture stand for 5 minutes to soften cereal. Add oil, egg, brown sugar and vanilla and stir until very well mixed. Stir in cocoa, baking soda and salt and mix. Add the flour and stir only until it is mixed. Stir in chocolate chips and divide evenly among the 10 muffin cups bake for 15-20 minutes depending on oven.

Remove muffins from the pan and let sit for a few minutes before serving. Serve warm.

Makes 12 servings.

NUTRITIONAL VALUE

1 muffin (serving): 210 calories, N.A sodium, 7g fat, 31g carbs, 4g fiber, 4g protein

SmartPoints Value: 9

Breakfast Yogurt Parfait in a Jar

A tasty, quick and easy way to start your day. The fruits can be swapped out for seasonal fruits or your favorite fruits on the accepted list.

INGREDIENTS

1 cup grapes or mixed berries

1/2 banana, chopped

1/4 cup unsweetened shredded coconut

1/2 cup granola

1/2 cup nonfat or low fat Greek-style yogurt

DIRECTIONS

Place a layer of berries or grapes on the bottom of the jar, add a layer of yogurt, a layer of granola, a layer of fruit, another layer of yogurt and a layer of the shredded coconut. Cap the jar, and off you go with no hassle, no fuss.

Feel free to get creative and mix it up a bit with granola, sugar free jams, or any other item that is of nutritional value and will add the WOW factor to your breakfast on- the-go.

Makes 3 servings.

NUTRITIONAL VALUE

Serving Size: 1 cup 184 Calories, 7g fat, 23g Carbohydrates, 4g Fiber, 1g Sugars, 6g Protein.

SmartPoints Value: 9

Skinny Breakfast Sausage

Enjoy lean ground turkey and loads of spices - NO artificial ingredients. Get your taste buds taunted with this delicious breakfast. You don't have to miss out on that sausage breakfast and you will be amazed at the mouthwatering taste.

INGREDIENTS

1 pound lean ground turkey or chicken (hormone and cage free recommended)

1/2 teaspoon garlic powder

1/2 teaspoon freshly ground black pepper

- 1 teaspoon dried sage
- 1 teaspoon crushed red pepper flakes (more or less to taste)
- 1 teaspoon dried oregano
- Kosher or sea salt to taste

DIRECTIONS

Combine all ingredients in a large mixing bowl. Make sausage patties to desired size and thickness. I usually get about 8 patties. Uncooked patties can be frozen for up to one month.

Add patties to a large nonstick skillet and cook on medium heat until brown on both sides and cooked through.

Makes 8 servings (based on making 8 patties of sausage from one pound)

NUTRITIONAL VALUE

Serving size 1 sausage: 85 Calories, 4g Fat, 10g Protein

SmartPoints Value: 2

Potato, Apple, and Gruyere Tart

This is one for the collection. Savory, smoky and sweet, a gourmet decadence at its best, and only 7 points.

INGREDIENTS

4 potatoes, peeled and thinly sliced

1 apple, thinly sliced (same thickness as the potatoes)

1 small onion, thinly sliced

2 tablespoons freshly chopped parsley

2 tablespoons olive oil

½ teaspoon Kosher or sea salt

¼ teaspoon pepper

½ cup gruyere cheese, grated

DIRECTIONS

Preheat oven to 425 degrees Fahrenheit and lightly grease a 9-inch cake pan with olive oil.

In a large bowl combine the potatoes, apples, onion, parsley, olive oil, salt and pepper. Toss the mixture until well-coated with olive oil.

Pour half of the potato mixture into the prepared cake pan and then sprinkle with ¼ cup cheese. Pour the other half of the potato mixture on top of the cheese layer. Cover the cake pan with a piece of lightly greased aluminum foil (this will help the tart retain moisture and prevent it from sticking to the foil).

Bake for 40 minutes at 425 degrees. Remove foil and sprinkle with remaining ¼ cup of cheese. Bake for another 15 minutes or until golden brown. Cut into 6 equal slices and enjoy!

Makes 6 servings.

NUTRITIONAL VALUE

Serving Size 1 slice: 195 Calories, 7.3g Fat, 28.3g Carbohydrates, 4.6g Fiber, 5.5g Sugars, 5.3g Protein. Fat: 2.3 g .

SmartPoints Value: 7

<u>Blueberry Greek Yogurt Muffins</u>

INGREDIENTS

1 cup whole wheat flour

1 cup white all-purpose flour

1 teaspoon baking powder

1 teaspoon baking soda

¼ teaspoon salt

1 large egg

2 tablespoon canola oil

1 teaspoon pure vanilla extract

⅓ cup sugar

1 cup vanilla Greek yogurt

½ cup orange juice

1 ½ cups blueberries

Cooking spray

¼ cup powder sugar

1-2 teaspoons 1% milk

DIRECTIONS

Turn oven on to 400 degreesFahrenheit.

In a large bowl mix together flours, baking powder, baking soda, and salt. Make a well in the center and set aside. In a separate bowl lightly beat the egg then mix in the canola oil, vanilla extract, sugar, Greek yogurt, and orange juice.

Pour the wet mixture into the well of the dry mixture and stir just until combined. You don't want to over mix the batter or it will be tough. Gently fold in the blueberries.

Divide the batter among a 12 cup muffin tin sprayed with cooking spray. I found it helpful to use a cookie scoop. Bake for 15 – 18 minutes or until light brown on top and toothpick comes out clean when inserted into a muffin. Take out and let cool in pan for 5 minutes.

In a small bowl, mix powdered sugar with milk until glaze forms. Use more or less milk depending on the type of consistency you want. Take muffins out of pan and place on wire rack to finish cooling. Enjoy.

Makes 12 servings.

NUTRITIONAL INFORMATION

1 Muffin per serving: 156 Calories, 26g Carbohydrates, 3g Fats, 2g Fiber, 5g Proteins.

SmartPoints Value: 4

Low-Fat Cranberry Scones

INGREDIENTS

2 cup all-purpose flour (Use whole wheat flour to kick up the nutrition a bit)

2/3 cup dried cranberries

1 tbsp baking powder

1/4 tsp baking soda–

1/4 tsp table salt

1/4 cup sugar

1/4 cup egg substitute (I like Egg Beaters)

1 cup fat fat-free buttermilk

1/4 cup low calorie butter, melted (I used Brummel & Brown)

TO MAKE FAT FREE BUTTERMILK: Mix 1 tbsp vinegar or lemon juice + fat-free milk to make 1 cup & let stand for 10 minutes = 1 cup fat-free buttermilk

DIRECTIONS

Preheat oven to 400 degreesFahrenheit. Coat a baking sheet with non-fat cooking spray. I used the Pam Butter Flavor kind.

In a large bowl, mix the flour, baking powder, baking soda, salt and sugar; mix well and set aside. In another bowl, whisk together egg, buttermilk and melted butter. Stir wet ingredients into dry ingredients until just combined; fold in cranberries.

Drop 12 equal two-inch mounds of batter on prepared baking sheet about 1-inch apart.

Bake until tops just start to turn golden, about 12 to 15 minutes.

Makes 12 servings.

NUTRITIONAL VALUE

1 scone:(no actual nutritional info?)

SmartPoints Value: 2

Whole Wheat Carrot Muffins

INGREDIENTS

1 1/2 cups whole wheat pastry flour

1 tsp baking soda

3/4 tsp ground cinnamon

1/2 tsp ground nutmeg

1/2 tsp ground ginger

3/4 cup unsweetened applesauce

1/2 cup nonfat plain Greek yogurt

1/2 cup (packed) brown sugar

2 tbsp canola oil

1 egg

1 cup (lightly packed) shredded carrots

1/3 cup golden raisins

1/3 cup chopped pecans

12 pecan halves

DIRECTIONS

Preheat the oven to 375 degreesFahrenheit. Lightly coat the muffin tin with cooking spray.

In a medium bowl, whisk together flour, baking soda, cinnamon, nutmeg, ginger and salt.In a large bowl, combine the applesauce, Greek yogurt, brown sugar, canola oil and egg.   Stir together until the mixture is smooth.

Stir the dry ingredients into the applesauce mixture until combined. Stir in the carrot, raisins and chopped pecans.

Spoon the muffin batter into the prepared muffin cups. Bake for 7 minutes. Place one pecan half on top of each muffin. Bake until a toothpick inserted in the center of the muffins comes out clean, an additional 7 to 9 minutes. Remove muffins from the pan and allow to cool. Serve.

NUTRITIONAL VALUE

Serving Size: 1 Muffin. 178 Calories, 6.3g Fats, 31.2g Carbohydrates, 3.1g Fiber, 14.8g Sugars, 3.8g Protein.

SmartPoints Value: 5

Cheeseburger Hash Brown Cups

INGREDIENTS

20 oz shredded hash brown potatoes (I use the pre-shredded refrigerated kind such as Simply Potatoes or Reser's)

2 tablespoons olive oil

1 teaspoon salt

Black pepper to taste

¼ cup diced onion

1 lb 95% lean ground beef

1 tablespoon hamburger seasoning (I use McCormick brand – recommended!)

2 tablespoons ketchup

2 teaspoons yellow mustard

6 grape tomatoes, chopped

½ cup shredded 2% cheddar cheese

DIRECTIONS

Pre-heat the oven to 375 degrees Fahrenheit. Thoroughly mist 12 cups in a standard muffin tin with cooking spray and set aside.

Place the shredded potatoes in a large mixing bowl and drizzle with the olive oil. Add the salt and black pepper and stir to coat. Divide the coated potatoes into the prepared muffin cups and press the hash browns down and up the sides of the cups to form a well in each. Place in the oven and bake for 35 minutes.

While the cups are baking, mist the bottom of a large skillet with cooking spray and cook the onions over medium heat for a few minutes until softened. Add the ground beef and hamburger seasoning and cook, breaking up the meat with a spoon until browned. Transfer the meat and onions to a bowl and add the ketchup, mustard and chopped tomatoes. Stir to combine.

When the hash brown cups are ready, remove from the oven and divide the meat mixture evenly amongst the cups. Sprinkle the shredded cheddar over the piled meat in the cups and return the pan to the oven for an additional 10-15 minutes until cheese is melted and hash browns are golden brown. Allow to cool for 5 minutes, remove from pan and serve.

Makes 12 servings.

NUTRITIONAL VALUE

1 serving: 131 Calories, 11g Carbohydrates, 1g Sugars, 5g Fats, 10g Protein, 1g Fiber.

SmartPoints Value: 6 per 2 cups of 3

Bacon Egg And Hash Brown Stacks

INGREDIENTS

Cooking spray (2 sprays)

4 frozen hash brown patties, prepared without fat

2 large eggs

3 large egg whites

3 ounces Canadian bacon, finely chopped

1 tablespoon scallion, minced (green part only)

1/8 teaspoon hot pepper sauce (optional)

1/8 teaspoon table salt (to taste)

1/8 teaspoon black pepper (to taste)

8 teaspoons spicy ketchup, hot and spicy variety (optional)

DIRECTIONS

Coat a large nonstick skillet with cooking spray. Place hash brown patties in skillet; cook over medium heat on first side until golden brown, about 7 to 9 minutes. Flip patties; cook until golden brown on second side, about 5 minutes more.

Meanwhile, coat a second large nonstick skillet with cooking spray; heat over medium-low heat. In a large bowl, beat together eggs, egg whites, bacon, scallions, hot pepper sauce, and salt and pepper.Pour into prepared skillet and then increase heat to medium. Let eggs partially set and then scramble using a spatula. When eggs are set, but slightly glossy, remove from heat; cover to keep warm until hash browns are finished cooking.

To assemble stacks, place 1 hash brown patty on each of 4 plates. Top each with 1/4 of egg mixture and serve with 2 teaspoons of ketchup.

Season to taste with salt and pepper, if desired. Finely diced turkey bacon makes a nice alternative to the Canadian bacon in this recipe. Just make sure to cook the bacon before adding it to the eggs (could affect SmartPoints value).

Makes 4 servings.

NUTRITIONAL VALUE
SmartPoints Value: 4

Breakfast Burrito

INGREDIENTS

Pam cooking spray

2 teaspoons olive oil

2 scallions, chopped

1 green pepper, chopped (I skipped, but next time I am adding green chilies or jalapeños)

1 tomato, chopped

2 garlic cloves, minced

2 eggs

4 egg whites

1/2 cup low-fat cheddar cheese, shredded (I used WW Mexican blend shredded cheese)

2 tablespoons cilantro, chopped

1/4 teaspoon salt

1/4 teaspoon pepper

4 whole wheat tortillas

1/2 cup nonfat sour cream

1/2 cup salsa

DIRECTIONS

Preheat oven to 400 degreesFahrenheit.

In a skillet over medium heat, heat the oil and then add scallions, green pepper, tomato and garlic and sauté for 5 minutes. Add egg whites and whole eggs, cooking until eggs are scrambled (3-5 minutes).

Remove from heat and stir in cheese, cilantro, salt and pepper.

Place tortilla on plate and spoon in 1/4 of mixture, roll up and place seam down in baking dish sprayed with Pam. Repeat with remaining tortillas. Bake for 10 minutes and serve with sour cream and salsa.

Makes 4 servings.

NUTRITIONAL VALUE

SmartPoints Value: 4

There are so many gorgeous, delicious, tantalizing breakfast I could go on for pages and pages but try the ones listed and use different variations to add some excitement and spice it up a bit.

Chapter 2: Main Dishes

Most of the SmartPoints that you will consume during the day will come from your lunch and dinner, so it is important to make sure that you are eating meals that will provide you with the proper nutrition and that will fit into your daily SmartPoints allowance. The recipes included in this chapter are all excellent options that will allow you to stay within your SmartPoints budget while also truly enjoying your meals. Some of these recipes are kid-friendly, so you don't have to sacrifice your healthy options to accommodate your family!

Taco Casserole

Tacos are a fun treat to enjoy – and not just on Tuesday's! Blending tacos into the form of a casserole can turn a messy, finger-based dish into a sit-down, portable meal to be enjoyed everywhere. This recipe will "wow" guests at parties as well as your family members when you surprise them with this taco dish. Believe it or not, tacos can be an incredibly healthy main dish with the right ingredients. Full of fresh and juicy ingredients, this recipe, is a no-brainer for success.

Preparation time: 10 minutes

Cook time: 30 minutes

INGREDIENTS

2 ounces Tortilla Chips (usually around 24), plus additional for serving

1 tbs. Chili Oil (or olive oil and red pepper flakes)

1 Chopped onion

2 cloves Garlic, minced

1-pound Ground Chicken

2 tbs. Taco Seasoning

1 can Black Beans, drained

1 cup Hot Salsa

1 cup Shredded Reduced Fat Cheddar Cheese

Optional: Other toppings such as jalapeños, olives, banana peppers, refried beans, Spanish rice, etc. If your family has different ingredients that they enjoy in their tacos, feel free to add these as well. Make sure to adjust accordingly in your point system to avoid getting off track.

DIRECTIONS

Heat oil in a large skillet. Add onion and garlic and sauté until soft. Add meat and taco seasoning. Cook, breaking up the meat with a spatula, for approximately 5 minutes. Add beans and salsa. Mix the ingredients well and continue to cook until salsa thickens.

Line the bottom of a large baking dish with tortilla chips, pressing down on them lightly to break them into bite-sized pieces. Although the recipe calls for a particular chip, feel free to substitute for tortilla chips of your choice. Spread meat and bean mixture over the chips and add your cheese to the top of the casserole. Add sliced jalapeños or other toppings that you want to the casserole. Bake for 20 minutes or until cheese is melted.

Makes 6 servings.

NUTRITIONAL VALUE

1 serving: 435 calories, 11g fat (4g saturated fat), 917mg sodium, 8g fiber, 3g sugar, 57g carbs, 31g protein

SmartPoint Value: 6

<u>Traditional Hearty Beef Stew</u>

Beef stew is a classic, easy slow cooker recipe. The only requirements are the purchasing of the ingredients and a bit of light preparation before throwing it all into the crock pot or stock pot to cook. Beef stew is great as leftovers as well so making a large pot lets you enjoy your hearty beef stew all week long.

Preparation time: 10 minutes

Cook time: 2 hours

INGREDIENTS

1 ½ lb. Lean stewing beef cut into 1-inch chunks

½ lb. Chopped carrots

½ lb. Chopped parsnips

1 lb. Chopped red potatoes with skins left on

3 Chopped celery ribs

1 Diced onion

2 tbsp. Worcestershire sauce

1 tbsp. vegetable oil

2 cups water

2 garlic cloves, whole

1 garlic clove, minced

2 bay leaves

1 ½ tsp salt

1 tsp sugar

½ tsp pepper

1 tsp. Smoked paprika

¼ tsp. Ground allspice

2 tbsp. cornstarch

2 cups beef broth

1 sprig of rosemary

1 sprig thyme

DIRECTIONS

Heat your vegetable oil in a large stock pot or crock pot on medium-high heat. Add beef and brown it on all sides.

Add water, onions, garlic, smoked paprika, bay leaves, Worcestershire sauce, allspice, salt, pepper, and sugar. Add your springs of rosemary and thyme; you can toss the springs in alone or wrap in a bundle using cheesecloth and add. Cover and simmer for 90 minutes.

Add the potatoes, carrots, parsnips, and celery to the pot, as well as the remaining or additional beef broth you are using, until it reaches the desired consistency. Cook for an additional 45-60 minutes or until beef is fork-tender and can be shredded easily. The required cooking time will vary depending on the cut and size of your beef.

Mix the cornstarch with a small amount of cold water and stir together. Pour the cornstarch into the stew and bring it to a boil. Immediately turn the heat off and let rest before serving. The cornstarch will thicken the stew.

Makes 8 servings.

NUTRITIONAL VALUE

1 serving (1 cup): 233 calories, 719mg sodium, 6g fat (2g saturated fat), 24g carbs, 4g fiber, 6g sugar, 22g protein

SmartPoints Value: 6

Pizza Chicken

Yes, you read that right: this is a recipe for pizza chicken, not chicken pizza. Chicken makes a tasty, low-fat, protein-filled base for pizza toppings in this different but delicious recipe. The fact of that this dish is fast and very easy to prepare makes this a quick go-to on those busy nights.

Preparation time: 10 minutes

Cook time: 10 minutes

INGREDIENTS

5 oz. raw boneless skinless chicken breast cutlet

Dash each of salt and black pepper

¼ cup canned, crushed tomatoes

¼ tsp. onion powder

¼ tsp. garlic powder

4 slices turkey pepperoni, chopped to size desired

3 tbsp. shredded part-skim mozzarella cheese

Optional seasonings and toppings: extra salt and black pepper, fresh oregano, crushed red pepper

DIRECTIONS

Pound the chicken until it reaches 1/4-inch thickness, and season with salt and pepper.

Spray a skillet with non-stick spray, and bring to medium heat. Cook the chicken for 3-4 minutes and flip to the other side and cook a remaining 3-4 minutes, until cooked through.

Sauce: combine crushed tomatoes, onion powder, and garlic powder in a bowl. Add the optional extra salt and pepper if desired. Mix well.

With the chicken still in the skillet, top it with the sauce, and sprinkle with cheese. Add the pepperoni on top.

Cover your skillet with a lid and cook for 2 minutes, so that the sauce is hot and the cheese is melted.

Makes 1 serving.

NUTRITIONAL VALUE

1 serving: 272 calories, 633mg sodium, 8.5g total fat (3.5g sat fat), 6g carbs, 2.5g sugars, 1g fiber, 40.5g protein

SmartPoints Value: 5

Cauliflower Rice Stir-Fry

This recipe is incredibly low in SmartPoints and is very, very tasty. The egg whites added to the stir-fry provide plenty of protein, and the various veggies make sure that you will get ample vitamins. The cauliflower 'rice' is a very healthy and low-carb alternative to rice, and is just as (if not more) delicious!

Preparation time: 20 minutes

Cook time: 15 minutes

INGREDIENTS

5 cups roughly chopped cauliflower (approximately 1 medium head)

¾ cup egg whites

1 cup frozen peas

3 cups frozen stir-fry vegetables

¼ cup water

1 tsp. chopped garlic

1 cup chopped onion

1 tbsp. sesame oil

¼ cup thick teriyaki sauce or marinade

DIRECTIONS

Working in batches as necessary according to your blender, blend the cauliflower on pulse until it is in small, rice-like pieces.

Spray an extra-large skillet with non-stick spray, and bring it to medium heat. Scramble the egg whites until fully cooked (3-4 minutes), breaking it into bite-sized pieces with a spatula. Place the eggs in a large bowl, and cover it to keep them warm.

Remove the skillet from the heat, clean if necessary. Re-spray the skillet with nonstick spray and bring to medium-high heat. Add the frozen peas, frozen stir-fry vegetables, and the water. Cover the skillet with a lid and cook for 3 minutes, or until thawed. Add the onion, cauliflower, garlic, and sesame oil. Cook while stirring until the vegetables have mostly softened (6-8 minutes).

Add the egg whites and teriyaki sauce or marinade to the skillet. Cook while stirring until the dish is hot and well mixed (2 minutes).

Makes 5 servings.

NUTRITIONAL VALUE

1 serving (1/5 of recipe, about 1 ¼ cups): 145 calories, 455mg sodium, 3g total fat (0.5g sat fat), 21g carbs, 10g sugars, 5.5g fiber, 8.5g protein

SmartPoints Value: 3

Chicken Nuggets

Revisit your childhood with this recipe that is packed with protein and taste. Add some grilled vegetables for a complete meal, without adding to the SmartPoints value. This is a great, healthy option if you have children that are shy about trying your new diet dishes. Kids will always eat chicken nuggets and this way they don't know the nuggets are healthier than any other recipe!

Preparation time: 10 minutes

Cook time: 20 minutes

INGREDIENTS

¼ cup whole-wheat panko breadcrumbs

½ tsp. garlic powder

½ tsp. onion powder

1/8 tsp. black pepper

¼ tsp. salt

8 oz. raw boneless, skinless chicken breast and cut into ten nuggets

2 tbsp. egg whites

DIRECTIONS

Preheat oven to 375 degrees Fahrenheit. Using non-stick spray, coat a baking sheet.

Combine breadcrumbs and seasonings in a wide bowl, and mix well.

Place the chicken in another wide bowl, top with egg whites, and flip to coat the chicken.

One nugget at a time, shake the chicken to remove extra egg, then coat with breadcrumb mixture. Place the nuggets evenly on the baking sheet and top with remaining breadcrumbs if any.

Bake for 8 minutes. Flip the nuggets, and bake about 8 more minutes until slightly browned and crispy.

Makes 2 servings.

NUTRITIONAL VALUE

1 serving (1/2 of recipe): 179 calories, 377mg sodium, 3g total fat (0.5g sat fat), 7.5g carbs, 1g sugars, 1g fiber, 28g protein

SmartPoints Value: 3

Veggie Bean Burgers

This recipe is almost too good to be true: it is full of protein and vitamins due to the mushrooms, black beans, and vegetables and has an incredibly low SmartPoints value of only 2 points! Yet it still manages to be incredibly yummy. You can serve it on top of a salad without adding any points to the SmartPoints value. It can also easily be made into vegan by using a vegan egg substitute and nutritional yeast flakes instead of eggs and parmesan – remember to note the difference in points value if you take this route.

This dish is a great option for an afternoon barbecue, letting you enjoy a barbecue-type meal while sticking to your SmartPoints budget.

Preparation time: 25 minutes

Cook time: 30 minutes

Chill time: 1 hour

INGREDIENTS

5 cups chopped portabella mushrooms

1 tsp. chopped garlic

1 cup finely chopped onion

¼ tsp. each of salt and black pepper

1 15-oz. can black beans, drained and rinsed

½ cup fat-free liquid egg substitute

¼ cup chopped fresh basil

¼ cup all-purpose flour

¼ cup finely chopped, bagged sun-dried tomatoes (should not be packed in oil)

2 tbsp. reduced-fat Parmesan-style topping

DIRECTIONS

Spray the skillet with a non-stick cooking spray, and bring to medium-high heat. Add mushrooms, garlic, onion, salt, pepper. Cook while stirring until softened (10 minutes). Place the mixture in a large bowl lined with paper towel.

Puree the beans, egg substitute, and basil until mostly smooth.

Remove the paper towel from the bowl of vegetables and blot away excess moisture from the mixture. Thoroughly mix the bean mixture and flour into the vegetables. Stir in the sun-dried tomatoes and Parmesan-style topping. Cover the bowl and refrigerate until the dish is cooled and set (at least 1 hour).

Once cooled and set, divide the mixture into 6 patties (about ½ cup each). Clean the skillet if necessary, and re-spray. Bring to medium heat. Cook the patties until firm and lightly browned (3-4 minutes per side). Be careful when flipping the patties, so that they keep their shape.

Makes 6 servings.

NUTRITIONAL VALUE

1 serving (1 patty): 139 calories, 372mg sodium, 1g total fat (<0.5g sat fat), 24.5g carbs, 5g sugars, 5.5g fiber, 9g protein

SmartPoints Value: 2

Pistachio Chicken Salad

This dish is a great alternative to the traditional chicken salad. It provides a unique set of flavors and is very healthy, offering plenty of protein, fiber, and vitamins. With preparation time being only 10 minutes and no cooking required this is an excellent lunch option, especially when you're on the go and need something that will fill you up and that you will enjoy eating.

Preparation time: 10 minutes

INGREDIENTS

8 cups chopped romaine lettuce (about one 12 oz. bag)

1 medium pear

1 medium yellow peach

20 dry-roasted shelled pistachios

6 oz. cooked and chopped skinless lean chicken breast

½ cup blueberries

¼ cup fat-free or low-fat balsamic or raspberry vinaigrette

DIRECTIONS

Distribute the lettuce between two plates or bowls.

Chop the pear and peach, removing the core and pit. Distribute the chopped fruit evenly between plates/bowls. Chop the pistachios and add them evenly to the two dishes.

Divide the chicken and blueberries between the two dishes. Drizzle dressing over each salad.

Makes 2 servings.

NUTRITIONAL VALUE

1 serving (1/2 of recipe): 295 calories, 384mg sodium, 7.5g total fat (1g sat fat), 36g carbs, 23g sugars, 8.5g fiber, 26.5g protein

SmartPoints Value: 4

<u>Glazed Roast Pork Tenderloin</u>

If you would like to have some friends over to enjoy a nice meal, while making sure that you are keeping to your SmartPoints budget, then this is the dish for you. You can serve it with grilled or boiled vegetables – cauliflower or broccoli would work well – for a delicious side that won't add any more points to your overall points value.

Preparation time: 15 minutes

Cook time: 25 minutes

Marinate time: 1 hour

INGREDIENTS

Marinade:

2 tbsp. reduced-sodium or lite soy sauce

1 tbsp. Dijon mustard

1 tbsp. Worcestershire sauce

2 tsp. brown sugar (loose, not packed)

½ tsp. ground ginger

1 tsp. crushed garlic

Pork:

1 1-lb. raw pork tenderloin, with excess fat removed

Glaze:

¼ cup low-sugar apricot preserves

¼ cup jellied cranberry sauce

1 tbsp. balsamic vinegar

2 tbsp. seasoned rice vinegar

DIRECTIONS

Mix the marinade ingredients in a small bowl until sugar is mostly dissolved. Place marinade and pork into a large, sealable plastic bag; remove the air and seal the bag. Through the bag, gently marinade the marinade into the meat. Marinate, refrigerated, for 1 hour.

Preheat the oven to 425 degrees Fahrenheit.

Combine the glaze ingredients in a microwave-safe bowl, and whisk well.

Spray an oven-safe skillet with non-stick spray, and bring it to high heat. Add the pork, discarding excess marinade. Sear the meat evenly, rotating occasionally, until it is dark on all sides (about 5 minutes total).

Bake the skillet in the oven for 10 minutes. Spoon ¼ cup of the glaze (about 1/3 of the sauce made) over the meat. Bake further until the pork's center temperature reaches 145 degrees (5-10 minutes).

Remove meat from skillet, and let it rest for 10 minutes. Microwave the remaining 2/3 of the glaze until warm (about 30 seconds).

Cut the pork tenderloin into even slices and top with warm glaze.

Makes 4 servings.

NUTRITIONAL VALUE

1 serving (1/4 of recipe): 217 calories, 560mg sodium, 4g total fat (1g sat fat), 18g carbs, 14g sugars, <0.5g fiber, 24g protein

SmartPoints Value: 6

Turkey Chili

Chili is a classic comfort food. This recipe provides a low-fat alternative, with lots of protein and vitamins thanks to the turkey and plenty of veggies. It can be made as a vegetarian or vegan meal by substituting a meatless turkey option such as Yves Meatless Ground Turkey – check the points value to adjust your SmartPoints balance accordingly if using a substitute.

Preparation time: 20 minutes

Cook time: 3-4 hours on high heat, or 7-8 hours on low heat

INGREDIENTS

1 29-oz. can tomato sauce

1 15-oz. can red kidney beans, drained and rinsed

1 15-oz. can of chili beans (pinto beans in chili sauce), not drained

1 14.5-oz can diced tomatoes, drained

1 large onion, chopped

2 bell peppers (each different color), stems removed, seeded and chopped

1 cup frozen sweet corn kernels

1 cup frozen sliced or chopped carrots

1-3 can of chopped chipotle peppers in adobo sauce, with sauce reserved

2 tsp. chopped garlic

1 tsp. ground cumin

1 tsp. chili powder

1 lb. raw lean ground turkey

Optional seasonings and toppings: salt and light sour cream

DIRECTIONS

In a large bowl, combine all ingredients except for turkey. Add 2 tsp. of the adobo sauce from the chipotle peppers. Mix and coat the beans and vegetables with the sauce.

Put the turkey in a slow cooker, broken into small chunks. Pour the chili mixture on top and stir.

Cover the slow cooker and cook (3-4 hours on high, 7-8 hours on low), until veggies have softened and turkey is fully cooked. Stir well before serving.

Makes 12 servings.

NUTRITIONAL VALUE

1 serving (1/12 of recipe): 176 calories, 765mg sodium, 3g total fat (1g sat fat), 23g carbs, 6g sugars, 5.5g fiber, 13g protein

SmartPoints Value: 3

Grilled Cheese with Caramelized Onions

This recipe makes the perfect combination of gourmet and comfort. While it does have a SmartPoints value on the higher range for dishes in this book, with a points value of seven per serving, it is an excellent source of protein and is very filling.

Preparation time: 5 minutes

Cook time: 25 minutes

INGREDIENTS

1 stick of light string cheese

1 cup diced sweet onion

Dash each of salt and black pepper

1 wedge of The Laughing Cow Light Creamy Swiss Cheese

2 slices light bread

2 tsp. light butter or buttery spread

DIRECTIONS

Divide string cheese into thirds, place in a blender or food processor. Blend at high speed until shredded. If no blender is available, pull the cheese into shreds and chop roughly.

Spray a skillet with non-stick spray and bring to medium-low heat. Add onion and a dash of salt and pepper. Cook until caramelized, stirring frequently (about 20 minutes).

Place caramelized onion in a medium bowl and add Swiss cheese. Stir until mixed and softened, then add string cheese.

Divide the mixture evenly between the two slices of bread. Spread butter on the other side of each bread slice.

Clean the skillet, and re-spray. Bring to medium-high heat. Put the entire sandwich in the skillet, buttered side down.

Cook the sandwich until cheese has melted and bread is lightly browned (2 minutes per side), flipping carefully.

Makes 1 serving.

NUTRITIONAL VALUE

1 serving: 285 calories, 815mg sodium, 8.5g total fat (3.5g sat fat), 36g carbs, 7g 10g sugars, fiber, 16g protein

SmartPoints Value: 7

Apple BBQ Pulled Turkey

Who doesn't love a good BBQ? From childhood, BBQ has always been a "go-to comfort food that everyone in the neighborhood loved. The smell of a good BBQ brings people from all over the town together. Combining the southern comfort of good barbecue with high nutritional value that makes this meal completely guilt free; this recipe will make even the toughest BBQ critics raise an eyebrow.

Preparation Time: 5 minutes

Cook Time: 4 hours

INGREDIENTS

2 lb. boneless skinless turkey breast

1 tsp. cumin

1 tsp. chili powder

½ cup unsweetened applesauce

2 apples, sliced

1 onion, sliced

2 garlic cloves, minced

1 tsp. Salt

½ tsp. pepper

1 cup barbecue sauce

½ cup low sodium chicken broth

DIRECTIONS

Place the turkey, onions, and apples into the slow cooker

In a separate bowl, combine the barbecue sauce, cumin, chili powder, applesauce, garlic, broth, salt and pepper, stir well.

Pour the mixture over the turkey and cook on low for 4 hours.

Shred turkey using two forks when done.

Makes 8 servings.

NUTRITIONAL VALUE

1 serving: 215 calories, 712mg sodium, 3g fat (1g saturated fat), 22g carbs, 15g sugar, 2g fiber, 25g protein

SmartPoints Value: 4

Spinach, Artichoke, and Kale dip

Who says chips and dip have to be for parties only? This spinach, artichoke, and kale dip combine the traditional dipping flavors with the twist of health. Enjoying dip without an ounce of guilt is a feat like no other. This dip can be enjoyed with vegetables and approved WeightWatchers crackers, adding versatility and variety to the tastes.

Preparation time: 5 min

Cook time: 4 hours

INGREDIENTS

2 cloves garlic

1/2 Diced onion

28-oz Drained canned artichoke hearts

10-0z Chopped spinach

10-oz Chopped kale

1 cup Parmesan cheese – the good stuff

1 cup shredded part-skim mozzarella cheese

1 cup nonfat plain Greek yogurt

3/4 cup light sour cream

1/4 cup low fat mayonnaise

Salt and pepper to taste

DIRECTIONS

In your food processor, chop garlic, artichokes, and onion until finely diced.

Combine everything together in the slow cooker and mix well.

Cook on high for 4 hours. Add the salt and pepper as needed, for taste.

Makes 20 servings.

NUTRITIONAL VALUE

1 serving: 98 calories, 245mg sodium, 39g fat (2g saturated fat), 5g carbs, 1g sugar, 2g fiber, 6g protein

SmartPoints Value: 2

Stuffed Sweet Potatoes Southwestern Style

Sweet potatoes have always been associated with a healthy diet. Southwestern sweet potatoes create a sweet and spicy flavor that is nearly impossible not to love. The fresh ingredients make preparation quick and easy.

Preparation time: 10 minutes

Cook time: 1 hour

INGREDIENTS

4 small sweet potatoes

1 tsp. olive oil

1 small red onion, diced

1 clove garlic, minced

1 tsp. Ground cumin

½ tsp. Chili powder

1 cup canned, chopped tomatoes with juices

½ cup cooked black beans (canned beans work fine)

½ cup frozen corn kernels (or you can roast your own corn)

2 tbsp. fresh cilantro, chopped

Sea salt and fresh ground pepper for taste

DIRECTIONS

Preheat oven to 400 degrees Fahrenheit.

Place sweet potatoes on a baking sheet and place in oven for 30 minutes. Remove potatoes from the oven and stick with a fork several times in each potato; place potatoes back in the oven for another 30 minutes or until potatoes are tender to the touch.

While the sweet potatoes are baking, over medium heat, prepare a skillet. Add olive oil and onions. Cook for about 2 minutes until onions are softened, but not translucent. Add the garlic and cook for 30 more seconds, then combine cumin, chili powder, and just a pinch of salt. Add the tomatoes, beans and corn. Stir until combined; add the cilantro and season with salt and pepper to taste.

When serving, carefully (potatoes will be very hot) place on a plate and slice each potato down the middle and sprinkle a dash of salt over each. Add filling to the four potatoes, dividing equally among the four.

Makes 4 servings

NUTRITIONAL VALUE

1 potato (serving): 215 calories, 15 mg sodium, 2g fat (1g saturated fat), 43g carbs, 3.5g sugar, 8g fiber, 8.5g protein

SmartPoints Value: 6

Buffalo Chicken

Sticky, sweet, lip smackingly delicious chicken. Who says you can't enjoy these and not feel guilty?

INGREDIENTS

1 lb boneless, skinless chicken breast

1/2 cup hot sauce

1/2 cup reduced-calorie vegetable oil-butter spread

1/4 tsp celery seeds

1 tbsp white vinegar

1/2 tsp Tabasco sauce

1/2 tsp red pepper flakes

1/4 tsp black pepper

1/2 tsp cayenne pepper

1/4 tsp Worcestershire sauce

DIRECTIONS

For the sauce: In a small saucepan over low heat, mix together everything except the chicken. Simmer, stirring occasionally while you prepare chicken.

For the chicken: Bring water to a boil in a large saucepan. Cut chicken into strips and boil until cooked through. When cooked, put chicken in a serving bowl or dish. Pour sauce over chicken and let it sit for a few minutes.

Variation: Cut chicken into strips. Lightly coat chicken with sauce. Bake in a preheated 375 degreeFahrenheit oven for 15-20 minutes until cooked through. Remove to a platter and coat with remaining sauce.

Makes 4 servings.

NUTRITIONAL VALUE

1 serving: 136 Calories, 3g Fat, 24g Protein

SmartPoints Value: 6

Chicken Fried Rice

Weight Watchers twist on Chinese Food. Grab your chopsticks and enjoy this homemade, healthy, nutritious take on everybody's favoritetake-out.

INGREDIENTS

Cooking spray

4 large egg whites

1/2 cup scallions, chopped; green and white parts

2 medium garlic cloves, minced

12 oz boneless, skinless chicken breast, cut into 1/2-inch cubes

1/2 cup carrot, diced

2 cups cooked brown rice, kept hot

1/2 cup frozen green peas, thawed

3 tbsp low-sodium soy sauce

DIRECTIONS

Coat a large nonstick skillet with cooking spray and set pan over medium-high heat. Add egg whites and cook, until scrambled, stirring frequently, about 3 to 5 minutes; remove from pan and set aside.

Off heat, re-coat skillet with cooking spray and place back over medium-high heat. Add scallions and garlic; sauté 2 minutes. Add chicken and carrots; sauté until chicken is golden brown and cooked through, about 5 minutes.

Stir in reserved cooked egg whites, cooked brown rice, peas and soy sauce; cook until heated through, stirring once or twice, about 1 minute.

Makes 6 servings.

NUTRITIONAL VALUE

1 serving: 179 Calories, 3g Fat, 3g Fiber, 2g Sugars, 18g Protein

SmartPoints Value: 7

Cheesy Chicken Noodle Casserole

INGREDIENTS

2 cups macaroni, cooked

2 cups boneless, skinless chicken breast, chopped

2 cups cream of mushroom soup, undiluted

2 cup skim milk

8 oz low-fat cheddar cheese, shredded

DIRECTIONS

Preheat oven to 350 degrees Fahrenheit.

In a large casserole dish, combine macaroni, chicken breast, cream of mushroom soup, skim milk, and cheddar cheese, mixing well. Cover and bake for 35-45 minutes. Remove cover and bake for 10-15 minutes longer.

Makes 8 servings.

NUTRITIONAL VALUE

1 serving: 153 Calories, 4g Fat, 1g Fiber, 1g Sugars, 12g Protein.

SmartPoints Value: 5

Whole Grilled Snapper with Lime Pickle

INGREDIENTS

1 very big red snapper, 2-4pounds

3-4 tbsp good quality lime pickle

3 garlic cloves, sliced

4 tsp crushed coriander seeds

1 bunch of chopped dill

2 tsp cumin seeds

1 small crumbled dried chili

Olive oil

8 oz green tomatoes, sliced

1 bunch of fresh coriander, chopped, keeping the stalks and leaves separate

2 limes

1 red chili, thinly sliced

DIRECTIONS

Start by mixing and toasting the cumin, coriander seeds and dried chili for a couple of minutes in a dry frying pan. Grind the toasted spices together and add them to the lime pickle with the garlic, coriander stalks and dill. Drizzle in oil to make a paste.

Slash the whole fish a few times and smear generously with the mix, rubbing it into the sliced openings. Grill until cooked and charred, or alternatively you can cook it on a griddle.

Squeeze over some lime juice (be careful of the flames if grilling). Turn the fish over halfway through, basting it in more lime pickle.

Grill the green tomatoes. If you're doing it on the grill, cover the grates with foil if necessary, and lift higher off the coals if the fire it too hot. Top with chopped coriander and sliced red chili.

THERE WAS NO NUTRITIONAL INFO GIVEN FOR THIS RECIPE.

Spaghetti Squash and Turkey Bolognese

INGREDIENTS

1 large spaghetti squash

1 lb lean ground turkey

1 tbsp olive oil

1 onion, finely chopped

1 carrot, peeled and finely chopped

4 garlic cloves, minced

1 25 oz jar of marinara sauce

Salt and pepper to taste

DIRECTIONS

Preheat oven to 400 degreesFahrenheit.

Cut the spaghetti squash length wise, and spoon out all the innards and seeds. Lightly mist with olive oil or cooking spray, and sprinkle with salt and pepper. Place both halves, cut side down, on a baking sheet and roast for 40 to 50 minutes, or until the flesh is very tender when poked with a fork. Remove and allow squash to cool.

While squash is roasting, heat the oil in a large skillet over medium heat. Add the onion and garlic and sauté until translucent, about 5 minutes. Add the turkey and sauté until meat is no longer pink. Add the carrot and sauté until tender, about another 5 minutes. Add the marinara sauce. Decrease the heat to medium-low and simmer gently for 15 minutes to allow the flavors to blend, stirring often. Season as desired with additional salt and pepper.

Using a fork, scrape out the strands from the inside of the spaghetti squash, and divide evenly into 4 servings. Top with Bolognese sauce and serve immediately.

Makes 4 servings.

NUTRITIONAL VALUE

1 serving: 274 Calories, 4g Fat, 12g Carbohydrates, 3g Fiber, 4g Sugars, 23g Proteins.

SmartPoints Value: 7

Asian Shrimp Stir Fry

INGREDIENTS

1/2 cup low sodium vegetable broth

2 tbsp sweet chili sauce

2 tbsp low-sodium soy sauce

2 tsp cornstarch

1 tsp sesame oil

3 tbsp olive oil, divided

1 tbsp garlic, minced

1 tsp fresh ginger, minced

1 lb jumbo shrimp, peeled and deveined

2 cups broccoli florets

1/2 cup shredded carrots

1 cup sugar snap peas

DIRECTIONS

Whisk together the broth, sweet chili sauce, soy sauce and cornstarch. Set aside.

Heat 2 tbsp olive oil in a large pan or wok over medium low. Sauté the garlic and ginger for 2 minutes. Add the shrimp and cook until the shrimp is cooked through, about 3-5 minutes. Season to taste with salt and pepper, then remove from the pan and set aside.

Heat the remaining 1 tbsp olive oil in the pan. Cook the broccoli, carrots and snap peas for 3-4 minutes or until the vegetables are tender. Add the sauce and cook for 2-3 minutes, stirring constantly, until the sauce thickens. Return the shrimp to the pan and cook until the shrimp is hot. Serve hot.

Makes 4 servings.

NUTRITIONAL VALUE

1 serving: 232 Calories, 12.9g Fats, 11.5g Carbohydrates, 2.08g Sugars, 19.11g Protein, 9g Fiber.

SmartPoints Value: 6

Always remember – recipes are guidelines and you can mix and change where you would like to make it interesting, as long as you take into consideration your SmartPointsvalues and what you have already used for the day.

Chapter 3: Desserts

Following Weight Watchers SmartPoints plan does not mean that you have to avoid desserts completely. As long as you are fitting the dessert's points value into your daily allowance, or using your weekly allowance to accommodate the dessert, then you can reward your sweet tooth while staying within your SmartPoints budget.

Peanut Butter and Chocolate Stuffed Strawberries

This dish tastes like candy, but it's really quite healthy, and the peanut butter adds protein. Easy to make, it is also an excellent dish to bring to a potluck. It will be the hit of the party! This dish is vegan if you make sure to use a brand of semi-sweet chocolate chips that have no milk ingredients added.

Preparation time: 10 minutes

INGREDIENTS

¼ cup powdered peanut butter

2 tbsp. water

6 large strawberries

1 tsp. mini semi-sweet chocolate chips

DIRECTIONS

Combine the powdered peanut butter and water in a medium bowl. Mix until uniform, smooth, creamy, and thick. If it look as if more water is needed, add in 1 tsp. increments.

Remove the stems from the strawberries, about ½ below the stem. There should be an opening in each berry. Use a small spoon or another scoop to remove about half of the inside of each berry, so that there is room for the filling.

Put the peanut butter into the corner of a plastic bag, and cut the tip off of that corner. Pipe the peanut butter through the hole into the strawberries.

Gently press chocolate chips into the filling.

Makes 1 serving.

NUTRITIONAL VALUE

1 serving (entire recipe): 148 calories, 187mg sodium, 4.5g total fat (1.5g sat fat), 21.5g carbs, 11.5g sugars, 5.5g fiber, 10.5g protein

SmartPoints Value: 4

Simple Spice Cake Muffins

This simple and straightforward recipe is a tasty and filling dessert option. The spice cake flavor makes this dessert a particularly perfect recipe for Thanksgiving or Christmas events.

Preparation time: 5 minutes

Cook time: 20 minutes

Cooling time: 35 minutes

INGREDIENTS

1 box of moist-style spice cake mix (15.25 to 18.25 oz)

1 15-oz. can pure pumpkin (do not use pumpkin pie filling)

2 tbsp. powdered sugar

DIRECTIONS

Preheat oven to 350 degrees Fahrenheit.

Place foil baking cups in a 12-cup muffin pan or spray it with non-stick spray.

Combine cake mix and pumpkin in a large bowl, until totally uniform and smooth. The batter should be thick.

Place the batter into the muffin pan cups.

Bake the muffins, until a toothpick inserted into the center comes out mostly clean (about 20 minutes).

Allow muffins to cool completely – 10 minutes in the pan, 25 minutes out.

Sprinkle the powdered sugar over the muffins.

Makes 12 servings.

NUTRITIONAL VALUE

1 serving (1 muffin): 177 calories, 270mg sodium, 2.5g total fat (1g sat fat), 37g carbs, 21g sugars, 1.5g fiber, 2g protein

SmartPoints Value: 7

Banana Split Morsels

This recipe is so easy to make and tastes much more decadent than the SmartPoints value would lead you to think. Another great option for bringing to a party, each bite-sized piece is like a piece of candy.

Preparation time: 5 minutes

Freezing time: 1 hour

INGREDIENTS

1 medium banana, divided into 16 slices

2 oz. fat-free strawberry-flavored Greek yogurt

2 tsp. peanuts, finely chopped

DIRECTIONS

Place the banana slices on a large plate or platter. Top with yogurt then peanuts.

Freeze the slices until the yogurt is firm (about 1 hour).

Makes 1 serving.

NUTRITIONAL VALUE

1 serving (entire recipe): 182 calories, 37mg sodium, 3g total fat (0.5g sat fat), 34.5g carbs, 20.5g sugars, 3.5g fiber, 7.5g protein

SmartPoints Value: 3

Baked Apples

Of all of the desserts in this section, this one is the most unbelievable: it is sweet and delicious, and has a SmartPoints value of zero! The dish also looks quite decadent when served, so it would be a fantastic option if you are hosting a get-together with friends or family.

Preparation time: 10 minutes

Cook time: 45 minutes

INGREDIENTS

4 medium Braeburn or Rome apples

1 12-oz. can diet black cherry soda

¼ tsp. cinnamon

1 tsp. granulated Splenda No Calorie Sweetener or granulated white sugar

½ cup fat-free Reddi-wip

Optional topping: extra cinnamon

DIRECTIONS

Preheat oven to 375 degrees Fahrenheit.

Place cored apples in an 8" x 8" baking pan. Pour the whole can of soda over the apples. Sprinkle the sugar/Splenda and cinnamon over the apples.

Bakes until the apples are tender (about 45 minutes).

Put 2 tbsp. of Reddi-wip on each apple.

Makes 4 servings.

NUTRITIONAL VALUE

1 serving (1 apple): 104 calories, 10mg sodium, <0.5g total fat (0g sat fat), 27g carbs, 21g sugars, 4g fiber, 0.5g protein

SmartPoints Value: 0

Banana Chocolate Bread Pudding

This recipe is ridiculously easy and fast to make, given how delicious the end result is. It also provides a plentiful amount of protein, thanks to the soymilk and egg whites. It's also an excellent comfort food when it is served in mugs as suggested. The recipe can be made vegan, just make sure to adapt the SmartPoints value accordingly.

Preparation time: 10 minutes

Cook time: 5 minutes

INGREDIENTS

4 slices light bread

½ cup mashed banana

¼ cup fat-free liquid egg substitute

¼ cup light vanilla soy milk

Dash of salt

2 tsp. unsweetened cocoa powder

1 tbsp. mini semi-sweet chocolate chips

½ cup sliced banana

Optional topping: fat-free Reddi-wip

DIRECTIONS

Toast the bread lightly. Once cooled slightly, tear into bite-sized pieces.

Thoroughly mix mashed banana, egg substitute, soymilk, salt, and cocoa powder in a medium-large bowl. Add the bread pieces and 1 tsp. chocolate chips, stir gently to coat.

Using non-stick spray, spray two microwave-safe mugs. Divide the mixture between the two mugs.

Put the mugs in the microwave together, and cook until set (about 3 minutes).

Place the sliced banana and remaining 2 tsp. of chocolate chips onto the mugs.

Makes 2 servings.

NUTRITIONAL VALUE

1 serving (1 mug): 239 calories, 350mg sodium, 4g total fat (1.5g sat fat), 46g carbs, 18.5g sugars, 8.5g fiber, 11g protein

SmartPoints Value: 5

Rainbow Cookies

This is a fun and colorful recipe that kids will love and can be involved in the making of, and that you can eat without guilt, thanks to the SmartPoints value.

Preparation time: 15 minutes

Cook time: 10 minutes

INGREDIENTS

¼ cup reduced-fat peanut butter

¼ cup brown sugar (loose, not packed)

2 tbsp. granulated Splenda No Calorie Sweetener*

2 tbsp. light whipped butter or buttery spread, room temperature

2 tbsp. fat-free liquid egg substitute

2 tbsp. no-sugar-added applesauce

¼ tsp. vanilla extract

½ tsp. baking powder

1/3 cup whole-wheat flour

Dash of salt

½ cup old-fashioned oats

½ of a 1.69-oz package of Milk Chocolate M&M's, roughly chopped

*As a natural alternative to the Splenda, you can use Truvia. Halve the amount of the Splenda, since Truvia is about twice as sweet. If you would rather use granulated white sugar, the serving statistics would be: 192 calories, 27.5 g carbs, and 14g sugars. The SmartPoints value would then be 7.

DIRECTIONS

Preheat oven to 350 degrees Fahrenheit. Using non-stick spray, coat a baking sheet.

Combine the peanut butter, Splenda (or alternative), brown sugar, butter, egg substitute, applesauce, and vanilla extract in a medium bowl. Whisk thoroughly.

Add the baking powder, flour, and salt, and stir until smooth. Then fold in the oats and M&M's.

Scoop the batter onto the baking sheet in six evenly spaced mounds. Using the back of the spoon, flatten and spread the mounds into 3-inch circles.

Bake the cookies until a toothpick put into the center comes out clean (about 10 minutes).

Makes 6 servings.

NUTRITIONAL VALUE

1 serving (1 cookie): 179 calories, 169mg sodium, 7g total fat (1.5g sat fat), 24g carbs, 10g sugars, 2g fiber, 5g protein

SmartPoints Value: 6

Apple Pie in a Mug

Apple pie is easily one of the most traditional desserts in North America, and now you can enjoy this wonderful dessert and still follow your SmartPoints plan. This dish is easy to prep, fast to cook, and only needs to cool for ten minutes before it is ready to eat – and it's fun to eat it from a mug!

Preparation time: 5 minutes

Cook time: 5 minutes

Cooling time: 10 minutes

INGREDIENTS

1 medium Fuji apple, cored, cut into ½-inch cubes

12-15 pieces Red Hots Cinnamon Flavored Candy

2 low-fat cinnamon graham crackers, crushed (1/2 sheet)

2 tbsp. fat-free Reddi-wip

Dash of cinnamon

DIRECTIONS

Place the apple cubes and Red Hots into a microwave-safe mug, cover, and microwave for 2 minutes.

Stir well, re-cover, and microwave until apple cubes are soft (1-2 minutes).

Mix well, and allow the mug to cool.

Top with Reddi-whip, graham crackers, and cinnamon.

Makes 1 serving.

NUTRITIONAL VALUE

1 serving (1 mug): 140 calories, 44mg sodium, 0.5g total fat (0g sat fat), 47g carbs, 24.5g sugars, 3.5g fiber, 0.5g protein

SmartPoints Value: 3

<u>Chocolate-Espresso Mousse Shots</u>

A chocolate mousse recipe that is almost entirely fat-free can seem too good to be true. Finding a recipe for chocolate mousse, that is also delicious AND fat-free? That is something close to a miracle, but this recipe is just that.

Preparation time: 20 minutes

Cooking time: 0 minutes

INGREDIENTS

2 teaspoons instant espresso

1 tbsp. hot water

1 package(s) of fat-free, sugar-free chocolate pudding and pie filling mix (1.4-oz)

1 ½ cup(s) fat-free skim milk

1 ½ cup(s) fat-free whipped topping,

16 chocolate wafer(s), lightly broken

DIRECTIONS

In a medium sized bowl, mix together espresso with water until dissolved; cool to room temperature.

In a separate bowl, whisk together pudding mix and skim milk until well combined; whisk in espresso mixture then fold in 1/2 cup whipped topping.

Line up 16 shot glasses and spoon 1 tablespoon of pudding in each one; top each with 1 1/2 teaspoons of cookie pieces, 1 1/2 tablespoons of pudding and 1 more teaspoon of cookie pieces.

Garnish each with 1 tablespoon of whipped topping before serving. Yields 1 shot glass per serving.

Makes 16 servings

NUTRITIONAL VALUE

1 serving (1 shot glass): Nutritional info N.A

SmartPoints Value: 2

Chocolate Mint Bars

These filling, densely packed chocolate mint bars contain a surprising ingredient not usually associated with sugary treats – black beans. But with a slight twist, black beans have been added to this recipe to add a richer, more densely packed chocolate experience.

Preparation time: 10 minutes

Cook time: 30 minutes

INGREDIENTS

1 can (14-15 ounces) of black beans, drained and rinsed

½ cup sugar

¼ cup unsweetened cocoa powder

¼ cup butter, melted

3 large eggs

½ tsp. Salt

½ tsp. Baking powder

¼ tsp. Vanilla extract

¼ tsp. mint extract

2 tbsp. all-purpose flour

½ cup mini semisweet chocolate chips

3 tbsp. white chocolate chips

1 tsp. vegetable oil

4 crushed peppermint candies

DIRECTIONS

Preheat oven to 350 degrees Fahrenheit. Line an 8-inch baking pan with nonstick aluminum foil.

Combine the mint extract, butter, salt, beans, sugar, cocoa powder, eggs, baking powder, and vanilla in the bowl of the food processor. Process the combined ingredients on high until the mixture is completely smooth, scraping down the sides of the bowl several times. Add the flour and semi-sweet chocolate chips. Pulse a few times just until blended.

Scrape batter into the prepared baking pan spread evenly. Bake until a toothpick inserted in the center comes out clean, 25 to 30 minutes. Remove the bars from the oven and place on a wire rack to cool.

When the mixture is completely cool, prepare the topping. Mix white chocolate chips and oil in a small bowl. Microwave on high, stopping to stir every 20 -30 seconds until chips are melted. Be careful heating the white chocolate as it burns quite a bit easier than regular chocolate. After the bars are cooled, drizzle the melted white chocolate over the top. Sprinkle the crushed mints over the top. Let them cool completely before cutting; as they cool, they harden. Hanging onto either side of the foil, remove the entire slab of bars from the pan. Cut into 16 squares. Divide each square diagonally in half .

Makes 32 servings.

NUTRITIONAL VALUE

1 triangle (serving): 70 calories, sodium N.A, 3g fat, 9g carbs, 1g fiber, 2g protein

SmartPoints Value: 3

Coconut Banana Pudding

If you are looking for a creamy, mildly tropical dessert, look no further than this coconut banana pudding. Both coconut and bananas swirl together to create a smooth, decadent, lightly flavored dessert that is sure to please.

Preparation time: 60 minutes

Cook time: 15 minutes

INGREDIENTS

1 tbsp. and 2 tsp. small tapioca pearls

14-oz light and unsweetened coconut milk

½ tsp vanilla

¼ cup sugar

4 ripe bananas

DIRECTIONS

To soften the tapioca pearls, soak them for an hour in a small bowl of water.

While the pearls are soaking, combine the sugar, vanilla, and coconut milk in a small saucepan.

Cook on medium heat, stirring constantly. The sugar needs to be dissolved completely.

Remove the pan from heat source and let it cool for 10 minutes.

As the mixture cools, peel three of the four bananas and slice into lengthwise quarters before chopping into small chunks.

Place the milk back on the burner and add the drained tapioca pearls and bananas and cook on low heat.

While stirring the mixture, cook until it has thickened, usually around 5 minutes.

Let the mixture cool slightly before placing in the fridge.

Place in a fridge to chill, chop up the remaining banana before serving and place banana slices on top.

Makes 6 servings

NUTRITIONAL VALUE

1 serving (1/2 cup): 164 calories, sodium N.A, 6g fat (5g saturated fat), 30g carbs, 18g sugar, 2g protein, 2g fiber

SmartPoints Value: 5

Blueberry Tart

Sweet and packed full of blueberry goodness. Dessert doesn't have to sit on the hips, so enjoy!

INGREDIENTS

1 cup whole wheat graham cracker crumbs

1/2 cup walnuts, lightly toasted

1 large egg white

1 tbsp light butter, melted

1/2 tbsp canola oil

Pinch of salt

2 cups fresh blueberries

8 oz reduced-fat cream cheese, softened

1/4 cup fat-free vanilla flavored Greek yogurt

1/4 cup pure maple syrup, Grade A

DIRECTIONS

Preheat oven to 325degrees Fahrenheit.

Coarsely chop toasted walnuts in a food processor. Add graham cracker crumbs and process until the mixture looks like fine crumbs.

Whisk egg white in a medium bowl until frothy. Add the crumb mixture, butter, oil and salt; toss to combine. Press the mixture into the bottom and 1/2 inch up the sides of a 9 inch removable-bottom tart pan. Set the pan on a baking sheet. Bake until dry and slightly darker around the edges, about 8 minutes. Cool on a wire rack.

To prepare filling: Beat cream cheese, yogurt and 1/4 cup maple syrup in a medium bowl with an electric mixer on low speed until smooth. When the crust is cool, spread the filling evenly into it, being careful not to break up the delicate crust. Arrange blueberries on the filling, pressing lightly so they set in. Chill for at least 1 hour in the fridge.

Makes 12 servings.

NUTRITIONAL VALUE

1 serving: 153 Calories, 10g Fat, 5g Protein, 2g Fiber.

SmartPoints Value: 4

Weight Watchers Jell-o Pudding Fluff

INGREDIENTS

1 – 16 oz container Cool Whip, thawed

1 – 1 oz package fat free instant vanilla pudding mix

1 – .3 oz package sugar-free orange Jell-o

1 – 20 oz can crushed pineapple, not drained

1 – 16 oz can mandarin oranges, not drained

DIRECTIONS

In a large mixing bowl, beat together thawed Cool Whip, pudding mix and jell-o mix until smooth. Fold in crushed pineapple and mandarin oranges and mix until combined. Chill in refrigerator until serving.

Makes 8-10 servings.

Skinny Pumpkin Energy Bites

Get your boost from these delicious home bakes. For fall seasonal festivities, you could make these SmartPoints approved bites for your guests, and they won't even know they're healthy! Everyone loves pumpkin anything in the fall, so don't restrict yourself just because the holidays are approaching.

INGREDIENTS

1 cup old fashioned oatmeal (uncooked)

1/4 cup pure pumpkin puree

1/2 cup wheat germ

1/3 cup honey

1/2 tsp cinnamon

1/2 tsp pumpkin pie spice

1/3 cup white chocolate morsels

DIRECTIONS

Combine all ingredients in a large bowl and mix until well-blended and the texture is consistent. Scoop into one inch balls, and store in the refrigerator in an airtight container.

Makes 12-18 bites.

One-Point Cookie Balls

INGREDIENTS

1 cup Quick Oats

2 ripe bananas

1/2 cup mini Chocolate Peanut Butter Cups, smashed up

DIRECTIONS

Preheat oven to 35o degrees Fahrenheit.

Combine all ingredients in mixing bowl and mix thoroughly. Scoop out 1-1.5 tbsp dough, mold into balls and place on cookie sheet. Bake only 15 minutes.

NUTRITIONAL VALUE

SmartPoints Value: 1 (per ball)

Pudding Pops

INGREDIENTS

1 package Chocolate or Vanilla FAT FREE, sugar free, instant pudding mix.

2 cups 2% milk

DIRECTIONS

Mix well, pour into molds and freeze.

NUTRITIONAL VALUE

SmartPoints Value: 1 point each

Skinny Key Lime Pie Pops

INGREDIENTS

Key Lime Yogurt Filling:

2 - 5.3 oz. cartons of Yoplait Greek 100 Calorie Yogurt, Key Lime flavor

4 tablespoons of Cool Whip Lite

Graham Cracker Crumb Crust:

3 tablespoons Keebler Graham Cracker Crumbs

1/2 packet of Splenda (optional & to taste)

6 sprays of spray butter

DIRECTIONS

Stir together both cartons of yogurt and Cool Whip Lite until smooth and combined. Divide yogurt mixture into 6 small paper cups (or a popsicle mold).

Stir together graham cracker crumbs and Splenda. Spray butter and stir to combine. Sprinkle 1/6 mixture of the crumb mixture over each popsicle and lightly press the crumbs into yogurt with the back of a spoon. Insert a popsicle stick into each popsicle and place in freezer.

Makes 6 servings.

NUTRITIONAL VALUE

SmartPoints Value: 1 per pop

Skinny Apple Cinnamon Monkey Bread

INGREDIENTS

Cooking spray (with flour in it)

3 cups apples, peeled and diced small

2 tbsp sugar

2 tsp cinnamon

⅓ cup reduced-fat butter or Smart Balance Light

¾ cup brown sugar

2 tsp water

1 tsp vanilla

3 tbsp granulated sugar

2 tsp cinnamon

2 – 12 oz cans Pillsbury refrigerated buttermilk biscuits or Pillsbury Golden Layer

Buttermilk Flaky Biscuits (100 calories for each biscuit)

DIRECTIONS

Preheat oven to 350 degrees Fahrenheit. Coat a Bundt pan with nonstick cooking spray.

In a microwave safe bowl, toss together chopped apples, 2 tablespoons sugar and 2 teaspoons cinnamon. Cook for 2 minutes to soften.

In the meantime in a pan, melt butter, brown sugar, water and vanilla. Bring to a boil, turn heat to low and cook for 2 minutes. Stir often. Set aside.

In a large bowl, blend 3 tablespoons granulated sugar and 2 teaspoons cinnamon. Quarter each biscuit from 1 package and roll each piece in about half the sugar/cinnamon mixture. Place biscuit pieces layered evenly in Bundt pan. Spoon ½ of cooked apples evenly over the biscuits. Spoon ½ of cooked sauce over the apples and biscuit pieces.

Quarter each biscuit from the second package and roll each piece in remaining sugar/cinnamon mixture. Place these remaining biscuit pieces layered evenly in Bundt pan. Add remaining cooked apples evenly over top of biscuits. Spoon remaining ½ of cooked sauce evenly over apples and biscuit pieces.

Bake for 25 minutes. Remove from oven, and let sit for about 5 minutes. While still hot, carefully loosen sides and middle of pan. Invert onto a serving plate.   Serve warm.

This dessert also freezes perfectly.

Makes 16 servings.

NUTRITIONAL VALUE

1 serving: 196 Calories, 7g Fat, 3g Protein, 34g Carbohydrates, 2g Fiber, 18g Sugars

SmartPoints Value: 8

Those of you on Weight Watchers don't have to give up delicious desserts just to eat smart. There are variations on a lot of popular dessert recipes, so don't limit yourself to only what you have found here. Do some of your own research and I'm sure you'll be amazed at what else you can find.

Chapter 4: Snacks and Appetizers

Whether you're hosting a party, attending a special event, or just feel like having a quick snack, there is no reason to deprive yourself of snacking throughout the day. The recipes for snacks and appetizers set out in this chapter are just some of the options that are available to you that will taste great and fit into your SmartPoints budget.

Tropical Pico de Gallo

This simple and delicious recipe is an excellent side, perfect for a summer picnic, and has a SmartPoints value of zero! It can be eaten with chips or as a topping for other dishes.

Preparation time: 15 minutes

INGREDIENTS

½ cup chopped mango

1/3 cup seeded and chopped tomatoes

½ cup canned black beans, drained and rinsed

¼ cup finely chopped red bell pepper

¼ cup finely chopped red onion

1 tbsp. seeded and chopped jalapeño pepper

2 tsp. lime juice

1 tbsp. chopped cilantro

¹/₈ tsp. black pepper

¼ tsp. salt

¹/₈ ground cumin

DIRECTIONS

Combine all ingredients in a medium-large, sealable container. Mix ingredients until uniform.

Seal container and refrigerate ingredients until ready to serve.

Makes 8 servings.

NUTRITIONAL VALUE

1 serving (1/8 of recipe): 25 calories, 108mg sodium, 0g total fat (0g sat fat), 5.5g carbs, 2g sugars, 1g fiber, 1g protein

SmartPoints Value: 0

Baked Onion Rings (Low-Fat)

The smell of onion rings reminds people of sports bars and carnivals. The light batter over fresh, cooked onions is nearly impossible to ignore. Having a low-fat onion ring option seems too good to be true, but Weight Watchers has one – and it is delicious.

Preparation time: 1-2 hours

Cook time: 12 minutes

INGREDIENTS

1 medium onion, sliced into several 1/4 inch rings

2 ¼ cups low-fat buttermilk

1/2 cup panko bread crumbs

1/4 cup whole wheat Italian seasoned bread crumbs

1/4 cup crushed corn flakes

salt to taste

olive oil cooking spray

DIRECTIONS

Lay slices of onion into a shallow dish. Pour buttermilk over the top and let soak for about 1–2 hours, refrigerated.

Preheat oven to 450 degrees Fahrenheit. Line a baking sheet with parchment paper.

Combine the panko, bread crumbs and corn flakes and place around half of the crumbs in a large dish, season with salt. Set the rest to the side to use when the first batch is all gone. This should help avoid clumping, and they should stick better to the onions.

Dip the soaked onion rings into the crumb mixture coating them well. Place rings onto two cookie sheets. Spray with oil and bake for around 12 minutes or until golden brown. Serve immediately while hot.

Makes 2 servings

NUTRITIONAL VALUE

1 serving size (1/2 onion): 75 calories, 0.6g fat, 15g carbs, 2g fiber, 3g protein, 2g sugar, 53 mg sodium

SmartPoints Value: 2

Zucchini Tots

What is healthier than tater tots? Zucchini tots! This interesting spin on the tater tot adds unique flavor and nutrition to an otherwise bland tot. This recipe gives you your vegetable servings for the day disguised as a battered, yummy substitute.

Preparation time: 15 minutes

Cook time: 15 minutes

INGREDIENTS

2 large zucchinis, shredded

1/2 small onion, shredded

1 large egg

1 tsp. garlic powder

1 tbsp. whole wheat flour

1/4 cup grated Parmesan cheese

1/3 cup whole wheat Panko breadcrumbs

Salt and pepper to taste

DIRECTIONS

Preheat oven to 400 degrees Fahrenheit. Spray a 24-cup mini muffin pan with cooking spray or use oil on a paper towel to wipe the inside of the cups with oil.

Place shredded zucchini in a cheesecloth or thin dishtowel and squeeze out excess liquid.

Add the zucchini and the remaining ingredients into a medium sized bowl and mix well, making sure everything is mixed thoroughly.

Scoop or spoon zucchini into muffin pan and bake in the oven for about 15 minutes or until golden brown. You should be able to get around 18 cups filled.

Remove from oven and cool for at least 5 minutes. With the help of a small spoon, run it around the outer edges of the zucchini tot to help break the tot away from the pan, then gently scoop it out and place on a dish or a plate to serve.

Makes 6 servings.

NUTRITIONAL VALUE

3 tots (1 serving): 75 calories, 2.5g fat, 8g carbs, 4.5g protein, 1.5g fiber

SmartPoints Value: 2

Buffalo Chicken Dip

One of the most popular go-to dips is the well-known buffalo chicken dip. This dip is popular at parties, get-together, and potluck parties. Nothing beats homemade, including homemade buffalo chicken dip, giving it a fresh and light flavor without nearly as much sodium as store bought dips.

Preparation time: 5 minutes

Cook time: 3-4 hours

INGREDIENTS

4-oz reduced fat cream cheese, softened

1 cup fat-free sour cream

½ cup Franks hot sauce

½ cup of crumbled bleu cheese

1 tsp. white wine vinegar

2 cups (14 oz. raw) cooked shredded chicken

DIRECTIONS

Mix the cream cheese, sour cream, hot sauce, blue cheese and vinegar together until smooth. Add the chicken and place in the crockpot to simmer on low for 3-4 hours. Serve warm.

Makes 9 servings.

NUTRITIONAL VALUE

1 serving (1/3 cup): 107.9 calories, 4.9g fat, 5.4g carbs, 10.3g protein, 0g fiber

SmartPoints Value: 3

Chicken Fried Rice

Any recipe with the word "fried" in it begs the question of whether or not its Weight Watchers approved. It's hard to believe that anything fried could be allowed in any weight loss diet. The good news is Weight Watchers recipes allow for every type of food with the right ingredients and preparation. This chicken fried rice is made with low in sodium and is high in flavor.

Preparation time: 10 minutes

Cook time: 15 minutes

INGREDIENTS

Cooking spray

4 egg whites (large eggs)

½ cup scallions, chopped. Use green and white parts

2 garlic cloves, medium, minced

12-oz boneless skinless chicken breast cut into ½ inch cubes

½ diced carrots

2 cups cooked brown rice, kept warm

½ cup frozen green peas, thawed

3 tbsp. soy sauce, low-sodium

DIRECTIONS

In a large nonstick skillet, coat with nonstick cooking spray and place the pan onto the burner over a high-medium heat.

Add egg whites and cook, scrambling them and stirring regularly every few minutes. Once cooked, remove from heat and place over to the side.

Recoat the skillet with pan spray off the heat before placing the pan back over medium-high heat. Add the scallions and garlic and sauté for 2 minutes. Add the chicken and carrots then sauté until the chicken is golden brown and cooked through; this usually takes around 5 minutes.

Stir in the previously cooked egg whites. Then add the cooked rice, peas, and low-sodium soy sauce and cook until heated thoroughly, frequently stirring every few minutes.

Makes 6 servings.

NUTRITIONAL VALUE

1 serving (194 g): 179 calories, 403mg sodium, 2g fat (0g saturated fat), 21g carbs, 3g fiber, 2g sugar, 18g protein

SmartPoints Value: 4

Buffalo Chicken Meatballs

Meatballs can be used in entrees, as an appetizer, or as a side dish. People often bring meatballs to parties. Not only are these meatballs a unique buffalo flavor they are also made with chicken which creates a lighter version of the classic meatball dish.

Preparation time: 10 minutes

Cook time: 16-18 minutes

INGREDIENTS

oil spray (I used my mister)

1 ¼ lb. ground chicken

¼ cup panko breadcrumbs

1 large egg

2 chopped scallions

1/3 cup finely minced celery

1/3 cup finely minced carrot

1 clove crushed garlic

kosher salt and freshly ground black pepper, to taste

1/3 cup Franks Hot sauce

OPTIONAL INGREDIENTS

1/4 cup skinny blue cheese dressing

finely chopped celery leaf for garnish

DIRECTIONS

Preheat the oven to 400°F. Spray a non-stick baking sheet with oil, lightly.

In a large bowl, combine the ground chicken, panko crumbs, egg, scallions, celery, carrot, and garlic. Season with salt and pepper, to taste. Wash hands and mix until well blended. Roll the mixture (1/8 cup each) into 26 round meatballs.

Place the meatballs onto the baking sheet and bake until cooked thoroughly or golden, usually around 16-18 minutes.

Place meatballs into a bowl and add buffalo sauce while gently tossing to coat everything well. Serve immediately and drizzle with blue cheese dressing, if desired.

Makes 26 meatballs.

NUTRITIONAL VALUE

1 meatball (serving): 37 calories, 2g fat, 1g carbs, 135 mg sodium, 0g fiber, 4g proteins, 0g sugar

SmartPoints: 2

Creamy Macaroni Salad

This dish is cool and creamy and provides plenty of protein and fiber. It is an excellent option to pack for a picnic or barbecue.

Preparation time: 20 minutes

Cook time: 15 minutes

Chilling time: 1 hour

INGREDIENTS

Salad:

6 oz. uncooked high-fiber elbow macaroni

2 cups bagged broccoli coleslaw

1 cup chopped red bell pepper

1 cup chopped celery

¼ cup chopped onion

2 tbsp. sweet pickle relish

6 large hard-boiled egg whites, chopped

Dressing:

¼ cup Dijon mustard

¼ cup plus 2 tbsp. light mayonnaise

1 ½ tbsp. white vinegar

1/8 tsp. salt

1/8 tsp. black pepper

1 no-calorie sweetener packet

Optional seasonings: extra salt and pepper

DIRECTIONS

Cook the pasta in a medium-large pot, according to package instructions (about 8 minutes). Drain thoroughly and place in a large bowl. Do not rinse.

Allow pasta to cool, then add the remaining salad ingredients and mix well.

In a medium bowl, combine the dressing ingredients and mix until uniform.

Add the dressing to the salad, tossing to coat. Allow to chill completely in the refrigerator (at least 1 hour) before serving.

Makes 8 servings.

NUTRITIONAL VALUE

1 serving (1/8 of recipe, about 1 cup): 144 calories, 341mg sodium, 3.5g total fat (0.5g sat fat), 21.5g carbs, 3.5g sugars, 3.5g fiber, 6g protein

SmartPoints Value: 4

Southwestern Guacamole

This guacamole recipe is a unique twist on the classic guacamole. With an ultra-low SmartPoints value of 2 per serving, it is a great choice to eat with chips or veggies, or use as a topping on other dishes.

Preparation time: 15 minutes

INGREDIENTS

8 oz. mashed avocado (about 1 cup, or 2 small avocados)

1 cup fat-free plain Greek yogurt

1 tsp. lime juice

¾ tsp. chili powder

¾ tsp. garlic powder

½ tsp. salt

¼ cup canned black beans, drained and rinsed

¼ cup finely chopped red onion

¼ cup chopped red bell pepper

2 tsp. finely chopped cilantro

DIRECTIONS

Combine the avocado, lime juice, yogurt, chili powder, garlic powder, and salt in a medium bowl. Mix the ingredients until uniform and smooth.

Stir in the pepper, onion, black beans, and cilantro.

Cover and refrigerate until ready to serve.

Makes 8 servings.

NUTRITIONAL VALUE

1 serving (1/8 of recipe, about ¼ cup): 73 calories, 180mg sodium, 4g total fat (0.5g sat fat), 6g carbs, 2g sugars, 2.5g fiber, 4g protein

SmartPoints Value: 2

Carrot Fries

While the initial reaction to the name of this recipe might be one of hesitation, one taste of the finished product will erase all doubts from your mind. As good as any potato fries, these carrot fries are high in vitamin A, and the recipe has a SmartPoints value of zero so you can eat them without guilt!

Preparation time: 10 minutes

INGREDIENTS

1 ½ lbs. peeled carrots (about 8 large)

¼ tsp. coarse salt, or more to taste if desired

DIRECTIONS

Preheat the oven to 425 degrees Fahrenheit. Using non-stick spray, coat two baking sheets.

Cut carrots into French-fry-shaped pieces. Place them evenly on the baking sheets. Sprinkle with salt.

Bake for 15 minutes

Flip the spears and bake for about 15 more minutes, until the fries are tender on the inside and slightly crispy on the outside. Note that thicker fries will take longer to cook.

Makes 2 servings.

NUTRITIONAL VALUE

1 serving (1/2 of recipe): 116 calories, 428mg sodium, 1g total fat (0g sat fat), 27g carbs, 13g sugars, 8g fiber, 2.5g protein

Spiralized Summer Rolls with Hoisin Peanut Sauce

These quick summer rolls made with carrots and cucumbers are a simple and creative spin on an ethnic dish. This light meal has a nutty twist to a mildly tasting dish while also adding a bit of spice. A mix of cilantro, basil and mint make for a fresh tasting dish to enjoy on warm, summer days.

Preparation time: 10 minutes

Cook time: 0 minutes

INGREDIENTS

FOR THE HOISIN PEANUT SAUCE:

2 tbsp. creamy peanut butter

2 tsp. reduced-sodium soy sauce*

1 tbsp. hoisin sauce*

1 tsp. Sriracha

½ tsp. Grated ginger

4 tbsp. warm water, to thin

FOR THE BOWLS

24 jumbo peeled and cooked shrimp

2 large English cucumbers

1 thick carrot (I used 8 oz)

1 cup shredded red cabbage

2 tbsp. cilantro leaves

12 basil leaves

12 mint leaves

2 tbsp. chopped peanuts

DIRECTIONS

Mix all of the sauce ingredients in a small bowl and refrigerate until ready to use. Spiralize the cucumbers and carrots, then cut into 6-inch lengths. Divide the cucumbers, carrot, and red cabbage between 4 bowls. Top each with 6 shrimp, 2 tbsp peanut dressing, fresh herbs and chopped peanuts.

Makes 4 servings.

NUTRITIONAL VALUE

1 serving (1 bowl): 164 calories, 7g fat, 65mg sodium, 382mg carbs, 15g fiber, 4g sugar, 12g protein

SmartPoint Value: 4

Bacon-Wrapped BBQ Shrimp

The name of this dish might make you think that this recipe can't possibly belong in a book about healthy SmartPoints recipes, but you would be wrong. This dish provides a lot of protein and has an unbelievable SmartPoints value of four per four shrimp. This is the perfect appetizer for a backyard barbecue, and no one will ever know that they're actually eating healthy.

Preparation time: 15 minutes

Cook time: 15 minutes

INGREDIENTS

$1/3$ cup canned tomato sauce

1 tbsp. apple cider vinegar

3 tbsp. ketchup

1 tbsp. brown sugar (loose, not packed)

½ tsp. garlic powder

8 slices of center-cut turkey bacon or pork bacon, halved widthwise

16 raw large shrimp, peeled, with tails and veins removed – do not use jumbo shrimp

DIRECTIONS

Preheat oven to 425 degrees Fahrenheit. Using non-stick spray, coat a baking sheet.

Combine tomato sauce, vinegar, ketchup, garlic powder, and sugar in a medium bowl and mix thoroughly.

Coat the sauce mixture over each half-slice of bacon. Wrap each bacon slice around a shrimp, and put it on the baking sheet, seam side down.

Bake the shrimp until they are cooked through (10-15 minutes).

Makes 4 servings.

NUTRITIONAL VALUE

1 serving (4 shrimp, ¼ of recipe): 154 calories, 612mg sodium, 5.5g total fat (2g sat fat), 6.5g carbs, 5g sugars, <0.5g fiber, 16.5g protein

SmartPoints Value: 4

Chunky Chicken and Veggie Soup

This soup is a comfort food, perfect for a cold winter afternoon. The chicken and beans provide lots of protein, and the vegetables will give you a good serving of vitamins for the day. The cook time is longer, but your house will smell delicious by the time the soup is ready to eat. Since you'll be using a slow cooker, this is a great option to prep and head off to work or to school, knowing dinner will be ready when you get home! At a SmartPoints value of two per cup, you cannot go wrong with this chicken soup recipe.

Preparation time: 20 minutes

Cook time: 3-4 hours (high heat) or 7-8 hours (low heat)

INGREDIENTS

1 ½ lbs. raw boneless skinless chicken breasts, cut in half

1/8 tsp. black pepper

½ tsp. salt

2 14.5-oz. cans (3 ½ cups) fat-free chicken broth

1 14.5-oz can stewed tomatoes, not drained

1 15-oz can cannellini beans (white kidney beans), drained and rinsed

2 carrots, chopped

2 cups bagged coleslaw mix

1 cup frozen peas

1 small onion, finely diced

¼ tsp. ground thyme

1 dried bay leaf

DIRECTIONS

Season the chicken with black pepper and ¼ tsp. of salt. Place all ingredients, except for remaining ¼ salt, in a slow cooker and stir to mix. Cover the slow cooker and cook (3-4 hours on high, 7-8 hours on low) until chicken is fully cooked.

Remove the bay leaf, discard. Place the chicken into a large bowl, and shred it using two forks – one to hold it in place, the other to scrape across the chicken and shred it.

Take the shredded chicken and remaining ¼ tsp. of salt, and stir them into the soup in the slow cooker. Serve when you are ready to eat.

Makes 10 servings.

NUTRITIONAL VALUE

1 serving (1/10 of recipe, about 1 cup): 150 calories, 570mg sodium, 1g total fat (0.5g sat fat), 15g carbs, 5g sugars, 4.25g fiber, 20.5g protein

SmartPoints Value: 2

<u>Onion Rings</u>

While it may be difficult to believe that onion rings can be healthy and fit into your SmartPoints budget, this recipe is actually incredibly low in SmartPoints at only two points for the entire recipe of approximately 30 onion rings. That makes this recipe irresistible – and on top of that, the onion rings are delicious! It also has a good amount of fiber and protein, so it is nutritious as well as delicious and healthy.

Preparation time: 20 minutes

Cook time: 25 minutes

INGREDIENTS

1 large onion

½ cup Fiber One Original bran cereal

$1/8$ onion powder, or more to taste if desired

¼ tsp. garlic powder, or more to taste if desired

$1/8$ salt, or more to taste if desired

Dash of black pepper

½ cup fat-free liquid egg substitute

DIRECTIONS

Preheat oven to 375 degrees Fahrenheit. Using non-stick spray, coat two baking sheets.

Cut off ends of onion and remove the outer layer. Cut the onion into ½-inch-wide slices, and separate the slices into rings.

Using a blender or food processor, grind the cereal into crumbs. Place them in a wide bowl and mix in the seasonings.

Put the egg substitute in a different wide bowl. Dip the rings into the egg substitute, shake to remove excess, and coat the rings with crumbs. Lay the rings on a baking sheet, distributed evenly.

Bake the rings for 10 minutes, flip, and bake further until inside is soft and outside is crispy (10-15 minutes).

Makes 1 serving.

NUTRITIONAL VALUE

1 serving (entire recipe): 155 calories, 515mg sodium, 1g total fat (0g sat fat), 41g carbs, 7g sugars, 16g fiber, 9g protein

SmartPoints Value: 2

<u>Chicken Quinoa Soup with Kale</u>

A lot of people believe Kale to be an acquired taste. Arguably so, Kale goes great with a variety of different recipes, including soups. Adding quinoa into the mix, this fresh-tasting soup is a crowd pleaser and is sure to warm you up on the coldest of days and refresh you on warm summer nights. This recipe works well for almost any occasion or as a side dish to almost any entrée.

Preparation time: 10 minutes

Cook time: 8 hours

INGREDIENTS

2 lbs. boneless skinless chicken thighs

1 cup dry quinoa

4 cups kale, chopped

3 ribs celery, chopped

3 carrots, chopped

2 poblano peppers

1 onion, chopped finely

6 garlic cloves, minced

8 cups low sodium chicken broth

½ tsp. cumin

½ tsp. dried thyme

Salt and pepper to taste

DIRECTIONS

Add everything into the slow cooker and cook on low for 8 hours.

Makes 8 servings.

NUTRITIONAL VALUE

1 serving (1.25 cup): 284 calories, 294mg sodium, 7g fat (2g saturated fat), 26g carbs, 4g fiber, 2g sugar, 31g protein.

SmartPointsValue: 5

Zucchini Chips

An amazing healthy, clean, and tasty snack and best of all only 1 SmartPoints value.

INGREDIENTS

2 Large Zucchini

Olive Oil

Sea Salt

DIRECTIONS

Slice zucchinis thin. Lay on a cookie sheet covered with foil. Sprinkle lightly with olive oil and sea salt. Bake at 250 degrees Fahrenheit for an hour. Flip them over and bake for another hour. Make sure they are dry and crisp.

Feta Stuffed Mushrooms

INGREDIENTS

20 mushrooms (about 1 pound)

1 tbsp butter

4oz crumbled reduced fat feta cheese

3 oz reduced fat cream cheese, softened

DIRECTIONS

Preheat broiler. Remove stems from mushrooms and chop stems. Set whole mushroom caps aside.

Cook stems, stirring in butter on medium heat for a few minutes (until tender). Add in feta cheese and cream cheese. Mix well and cook until cream cheese is melted. Spoon evenly into mushroom caps and place on broiler pan. Broil 3 minutes or until golden brown; serve warm.

Baked Parmesan Green Bean Fries

INGREDIENTS

1lb fresh green beans, washed and trimmed

1/4 cup grated Parmesan cheese

1/4 cup Panko breadcrumbs

2 tsp garlic powder

Salt and pepper to taste

DIRECTIONS

Preheat oven to 425 degreesFahrenheit. Line a large baking sheet with foil and spray with an olive oil mister, or non-fat cooking spray.

In a small bowl, combine the parmesan, Panko, garlic powder and salt and pepper. Place green beans on baking sheet, making sure they are spread out evenly and not overlapping. Mist them lightly with an olive oil mister or non-fat cooking spray.

Sprinkle Parmesan cheese mixture evenly over all the green beans. Place in oven and bake for about 12-15 minutes, or until green beans are golden brown and begin to crisp.

Makes 4 servings.

NUTRITIONAL VALUE

1 serving: 77 Calories, 2g Fats, 11g Carbohydrates, 5g Protein, 4g Fiber.

SmartPoints Value : 2

Chapter 5: Drinks

Whether alcoholic or non-alcoholic, cold or warm, drinks can and should be a part of your everyday diet. Using the information set out in this book about the following drink recipes, you will be able to enjoy these items while maintaining your SmartPoints daily allowance.

Shamrock Shake

If you are looking for a deceivingly healthy smoothie recipe to serve on St. Patrick's Day (or any other day, for that matter!), look no further. This recipe is a fantastic source of protein and has a SmartPoints value of only two for the entire recipe. It can easily be made vegan – just make sure to adjust the points value accordingly if you are substituting items. You could also make it a cocktail, again adding the applicable points to make sure that you are keeping in line with your SmartPoints budget.

Preparation time: 5 minutes

INGREDIENTS

¾ cup unsweetened vanilla almond milk

1 oz. (6 tbsp.) vanilla protein powder, with 100 calories per serving

¹/₃ cup spinach leaves

¹/₈ tsp. peppermint extract

1 ¼ cups crushed ice (or 6-10 ice cubes)

DIRECTIONS

Place the ingredients in a blender and blend at high speed until smooth. Stop and stir if necessary during blending.

Makes 1 serving.

NUTRITIONAL VALUE

1 serving: 133 calories, 210mg sodium, 4g total fat (0.5g sat fat), 6g carbs, 1.5g sugars, 1g fiber, 20g protein

SmartPoints Value: 2

Spiced Apple Sparkling Sangria

This is a fun and easy recipe that will be a hit at any party. With the option to soak apples overnight for better flavor, it is a great recipe to prep the night before the party, so when your guests arrive, all you need to do is add a couple ingredients and serve. The SmartPoints value of five per cup includes the whiskey and white wine, so you don't have to worry about adding points for the alcoholic portion of this yummy drink.

Preparation time: 10 minutes

Chilling time: 4 hours

INGREDIENTS

3 cups Gala or Fuji apples, thinly sliced and halved (about 3 apples)

2 cups light apple juice, chilled

1 cup cinnamon-flavored whiskey

1 750-ml. bottle dry, sparkling white wine, chilled

2 cups club soda, chilled

Optional garnish: cinnamon sticks

DIRECTIONS

Put the apples in a large pitcher or serving bowl – must have at least a 2-quart capacity. Stir in the apple juice and whiskey.

Cover the apples and refrigerate for at least 4 hours. Note that the longer that it soaks, the stronger the flavor will be.

Just before you are ready to serve, add the sparkling white wine and club soda and stir gently.

Makes 10 servings.

NUTRITIONAL VALUE

1 serving (1/10 of recipe, about 1 cup): 133 calories, 15mg sodium, 0g total fat (0g sat fat), 13g carbs, 11.5g sugars, 1g fiber, 0g protein

SmartPoints Value: 5

Chocolate Peanut Butter Banana Smoothie

This is another smoothie recipe that is full of protein and fiber, making it an excellent start to your day to use as a breakfast smoothie or a perfect mid-day snack. You can also add alcohol to make it at a cocktail, or make it vegan, adding in the proper points to the SmartPoints value.

Preparation time: 5 minutes

INGREDIENTS

¾ cup unsweetened vanilla almond milk

2 tbsp. chocolate protein powder, with 100 calories per 1-oz. serving

1/3 cup sliced, frozen banana

2 tbsp. powdered peanut butter

1 ¼ cup crushed ice (or 6-10 ice cubes)

DIRECTIONS

Blend all of the ingredients together at high speed until smooth. Stop and stir the mixture if required.

Makes 1 serving.

NUTRITIONAL VALUE

1 serving (entire recipe): 152 calories, 244mg sodium, 4.5g total fat (0.5g sat fat), 19.5g carbs, 9g sugars, 4g fiber, 12g protein

SmartPoints Value: 5

Spicy Hot Chocolate

This hot chocolate has a little extra kick that makes this drink especially comforting on a chilly day. It can easily be made into a vegan recipe by using a milk substitute and a brand of semi-sweet chocolate chips that doesn't have any milk ingredients added.

Preparation time: 5 minutes

Cook time: 5 minutes or less

INGREDIENTS

1 ½ tbsp. unsweetened cocoa powder

1 tsp. mini semi-sweet chocolate chips

2 no-calorie sweetener packet

Dash of cayenne pepper

¼ tsp. cinnamon

½ cup fat-free milk

½ cup very hot water, divided in half

DIRECTIONS

Mix the cocoa powder, sweetener, chocolate chips, cinnamon, and cayenne pepper in a microwave-safe mug.

Add ¼ cup of very hot water, stir until well mixed and dissolved.

Add the milk along with another ¼ cup of hot water, and mix well.

Microwave the mug and mixture until hot (about 45 seconds).

Makes 1 serving.

NUTRITIONAL VALUE

1 serving (entire recipe): 99 calories, 65mg sodium, 3g total fat (1.5g sat fat), 15.5g carbs, 9g sugars, 3g fiber, 5.5g protein

SmartPoints Value: 4

Piña Colada

This recipe has an unbelievably low SmartPoints value given how rich and creamy it is, and is also a good source of protein. The SmartPoints value is six for the entire recipe, or approximately two points per cup. You can also remove the alcohol for a non-alcoholic option, which would set the points value at less than one per cup.

Preparation time: 5 minutes

INGREDIENTS

3 tbsp. vanilla protein powder, about 100 calories per 1-oz. serving

¼ cup canned and crushed pineapple, packed in juice (not drained)

1 ½ oz. white rum

1/8 tsp. coconut extract

1 cup crushed ice (or 8 ice cubes)

½ cup water

DIRECTIONS

Combine all of the ingredients in a blender, and add ½ cup of water. Blend until smooth; stop and stir as necessary while in the blender.

Makes 1 serving.

NUTRITIONAL VALUE

1 serving (entire recipe): 183 calories, 35mg sodium, 0.5g total fat (0.5g sat fat), 11g carbs, 8g sugars, 0.5g fiber, 9.5g protein

SmartPoints Value: 6

Marvelous Margarita

This margarita recipe is exactly what you need on a hot summer day, lounging in the sun in the backyard. With a SmartPoints value of only four per serving, you can cool down with this guilt-free drink. The SmartPoints value does include the tequila, so you do not need to add any points to take the alcohol into consideration.

Preparation time: 5 minutes

INGREDIENTS

6 oz. diet lemon-lime soda

1 oz. lime juice

1 ½ oz. tequila

1 2-serving package sugar-free powdered lemonade drink mix (about 1 tsp.)

1 cup crushed ice (or 5-8 ice cubes)

Optional garnish: slice of lime

DIRECTIONS

Combine all ingredients except ice in a glass or shaker. Stir until drink mix is completely dissolved.

Pour the mixture into a margarita glass with ice. For a frozen version, add drink mix and ice cubes into a blender and blend until ice is well chopped.

Makes 1 serving.

NUTRITIONAL VALUE

1 serving (entire recipe): 115 calories, 55mg sodium, 0g total fat (0g sat fat), 2g carbs, <0.5g sugars, 0g fiber, 0g protein

SmartPoints Value: 4

Chapter 6: Vegetarians and Weight Watchers

Being vegetarian does not exclude you from Weight Watchers. Any vegetarian meal plan can fit into the Weight Watchers regime. The same points tracking system would be used for a vegetarian with the only difference being that you would leave out meat protein. Track what you do eat and should eat according to the plan designed for you which takes into account your gender, age, height and weight at the beginning. Meat protein substitutes such as tofu and veggie burgers are allocated SmartPoints on the Weight Watchers program.

Weight Watchers is after all not a diet, it is a healthy eating plan and lifestyle change, as is vegetarianism. One should still be careful of food choices as a vegetarian as too much of certain plant foods can hinder weight loss. Follow the points system strictly. Being vegetarian does not mean that there are no pre-written recipes for you to enjoy.

Couscous Pilaf

Change it up a bit. Choose couscous instead of rice, flavored with delicious spices and chunky fresh vegetables.

INGREDIENTS

1 tbsp olive oil

2 medium carrots, chopped

1 head broccoli florets, chopped

1 cup couscous

1 cup vegetable broth(reduced sodium)

1/2 tsp garlic powder

1/2 tsp onion powder

1 lemon, juiced

Salt & pepper to taste

DIRECTIONS

In a large skillet or wok, sauté the carrots and broccoli until the vegetables begin to become tender, about 10 minutes. If needed, add a little water to prevent the vegetables from sticking to the pan.

Add the vegetable broth and bring to a boil. Add the couscous, turn off the heat and cover. Let the couscous sit for 5 minutes then fluff with a fork.

Add the spices, lemon juice and season the couscous to taste with salt and pepper.

Serve piping hot to enjoy best.

Makes 4 servings.

NUTRITIONAL VALUE

1 serving: 218 Calories, 4g Fat, 39g Carbohydrates, 2g Sugars, 7g Protein, 3g Fiber.

SmartPoints Value: 6

Sandwich with Beet Humus and Greens

Enjoy a fresh sandwich with a dash of color and texture.

INGREDIENTS

4 slices whole grain bread

1 avocado, sliced

4 radishes, sliced

2 cups baby spinach

1 cup alfalfa sprouts

4 tbsp beet hummus

DIRECTIONS

Spread the hummus on the bread.

Top with the avocado, radishes, spinach and sprouts.

Top the sandwich with the other slice of bread and slice the sandwich in half.

Makes 4 servings (one serving is only *half* of a sandwich).

NUTRITIONAL VALUE

1 serving: 151 Calories, 8g Fat, 18g Carbohydrates, 3g Sugar, 5g Fiber, 5g Protein.

SmartPoints Value:5

Baked Ratatouille

A traditional French recipe of vegetables stewed and baked in herbs and spices.
Delicious aroma and bright attractive vegetable - an attack on the senses - gets your mouth watering.

INGREDIENTS

1/2 lb eggplant, sliced

1/2 lb zucchini, sliced

1/2 lb Roma or beefsteak tomatoes sliced

2 tbsp olive oil

2 cloves garlic, minced

Salt & pepper to taste

Pinch crushed red pepper

1/4 cup red wine vinegar

2 tbsp fresh marjoram leaves, chopped

1/2 tbsp fresh thyme leaves, chopped

DIRECTIONS

Preheat oven to 400 degrees Fahrenheit.

Lightly grease a Dutch oven or other oven-safe dish. Arrange the vegetables in the pan. In a small bowl, combine the remaining ingredients. Pour the seasonings over the vegetables. Bake for 45 minutes, or until the vegetables are tender. Season again to taste with salt and pepper.

Serve hot so you get the full sensory overload of sight and smell and then experience the taste.

Makes 6 servings.

NUTRITIONAL VALUE

1 serving: 68 Calories, 5g Fat, 6g Carbohydrates, 3g Sugars, 2g Proteins, 2g Fiber.

SmartPoints Value:3

Quinoa Stuffed Mini Peppers

A burst of color and flavor for a perfect party appetizer.

INGREDIENTS

1 cup quinoa

1 1/4 cups vegetable broth

8 cocktail tomatoes, diced

1/2 English cucumber, diced

6 green onions, sliced

1 lemon, juiced

2 tbsp mint, chopped

1 tsp ground cumin

1/2 tsp garlic powder

1/4 tsp black pepper

1/4 cup olive oil

1/2 cup fetacheese, crumbled

1 1/2 lbs mini sweet peppers, assorted colors

DIRECTIONS

In a medium saucepan, bring the quinoa and vegetable broth to a boil.

Cover, and reduce the heat to medium or medium low.

Simmer for 10 - 15 minutes, or until the liquid is absorbed and the quinoa is tender.

Remove the quinoa from the heat and allow the quinoa to cool while preparing the rest of the ingredients.

Cut the peppers in half and remove the seeds (removing stems is optional).

In a large bowl, combine the quinoa, parsley, tomatoes, cucumbers, green onions, lemon juice, mint, cumin, garlic, pepper and olive oil. Mix well.

Add the feta and mix until well combined.

Evenly divide the quinoa mixture between the prepared peppers.

Serve immediately or chill until serving.

For this recipe make sure your chopping skills are not rusty.

Makes 10 servings, where 4-6 halves is one serving.

NUTRITIONAL VALUE

1 serving; 170 Calories, 8g Fat, 21g Carbohydrates, 5g Sugars, 5g Protein, 4g Fiber.

SmartPoints Value:4

Banana Coconut Pudding

Light coconut milk with sweet banana pieces. Easy and delicious and nothing to feel guilty about.

INGREDIENTS

1 tbsp + 2 tsp small pearl tapioca

14 oz light, unsweetened coconut milk

1/2 tsp vanilla

1/4 cup sugar

4 ripe bananas

DIRECTIONS

Soak the tapioca in a small bowl of water for 1 hour to soften the pearls. Meanwhile, combine the coconut milk, vanilla and sugar in a small saucepan. Cook over medium heat, stirring constantly, until the sugar is completely dissolved. Remove the pan from the heat and allow it to cool for 10 minutes.

While the mixture is cooling, peel 3 bananas. Slice into lengthwise quarters and then chop into small chunks. Return the milk to the burner and add the drained tapioca and bananas over low heat. Cook, while stirring, until the mixture has thickened, about 5 minutes.

Allow the mixture to cool slightly before chilling in the refrigerator until cold. Serve with the remaining banana sliced over the top.

Makes 6 servings.

NUTRITIONAL VALUE

1 serving: 164 Calories, 6g Fats, 2g Proteins, 18g Sugar, 2g Fiber.

SmartPoints Value:5

Chapter 7: Vegans and Weight Watchers

Being a vegetarian or an even stricter vegan does not necessarily mean you are thin. Many vegetarians and vegans are troubled with excess weight. Vegans especially, due to the limited variety of foods they eat, will often eat foods which are not necessarily good for the waist line with the assumption that they eat only vegetable foods so they won't put on weight. This is not true, as many have found out for themselves.

Weight gain can affect anyone at any time and not always due to overeating but rather eating the wrong foods. Vegans are no different. For a vegan trying to shed a few pounds the Weight Watchers plan could do wonders. There are a vast number of zero points veggies available and as vegans eat almost only vegetables, this is the perfect way for them to curb any hunger. EAT ZERO POINT VEGGIES.

There are so many alternatives to replace animal products on the Weight Watchers plan. The main cause of weight gain in vegans is because they think they are not eating any animal products or byproducts or processed food, so they will lose weight by default. However, they don't realize that it depends what they replace those foods with. Weight Watchers and the SmartPoints system will help vegans get on the right path to making the right substitutes.

Vegan recipes on Weight Watchers are countless. You will find a few helpful recipes below.

13 Bean Soup Recipe

Glorious, warm and hearty and completely Weight Watchers approved. Curl up on a cold evening and sip on a cup of magic.

INGREDIENTS

2 cups dry bean mix (I used Bob's Red Mill)

1 large onion, diced

2 stalks of celery, diced

2 large carrots, diced

1 28oz can diced tomatoes

5 garlic cloves, minced

1 tbsp chili powder

1/3 cup cilantro, chopped

10 cups water

Salt and pepper to taste

DIRECTIONS

Day 1: Rinse beans, then cover with water in a large bowl, and let soak overnight. Drain and rinse beans.

Day 2: Bring the 10 cups of water and beans to a boil. Reduce heat to medium low and let simmer for about 2 hours or until beans are tender. Add in onion, carrot, celery, tomatoes, garlic, cilantro, chili powder, salt and pepper. Let cook for another 30 minutes. Serve.

Makes 8 servings; approximately 2 cups of soup per serving.

NUTRITIONAL VALUE

1 serving: 200 Calories, 1g Fat, 35g Carbohydrates, 12g Fiber, 2g Sugars, 13g Protein.

SmartPoints Value:5

Lemon Pepper Veggies

INGREDIENTS

1 tbsp olive oil

1 small red onion, chopped

1 medium zucchini, sliced

1 large yellow bell pepper, chopped

2 tomatoes, chopped

1 tsp lemon pepper

1 tsp dried oregano

1 tsp dried parsley

1/2 tsp garlic powder

Salt to taste

DIRECTIONS

Over medium high heat, heat the olive oil in a large skillet. Sauté the onion for 2 minutes. Add the zucchini and sauté for another 2-3 minutes. Add the bell peppers and tomatoes. Continue to cook until the vegetables are hot and beginning to get tender. Add the seasonings, and adjust to taste as necessary. Mix well and serve hot.

Makes 4 servings; 1 cup per serving.

NUTRITIONAL VALUE
1 serving: 71 Calories, 3.1g Fat, 9.4g Carbohydrates, 1.5g Sugar, 1.6g Protein, 2.5g Fiber.

SmartPoints Value:1

Vegan Quinoa Chili

Easy chili recipe that tastes just as hearty as any beef-based chili. Being vegan doesn't mean you have to eat bland, tasteless food.

INGREDIENTS

1 cup quinoa, uncooked

1 medium-sized yellow onion, finely chopped

1 – 28 oz can diced tomatoes

1 – 4.5 oz can green chilies

1 – 15 oz can tomato sauce

1 – 15 oz can black beans drained and rinsed

1 – 15 oz can kidney beans drained and rinsed

1 cup corn– frozen, canned, or fresh

1/3 cup cilantro, finely chopped

5 garlic cloves, minced

1 1/2 tbsp chili powder

1 tbsp ground cumin

1 tbsp paprika

1 tbsp olive oil

Juice of 1 lime

Salt and pepper to taste

DIRECTIONS

Cook quinoa according to package instructions and set aside.

Heat oil over medium high heat in a large pot or Dutch oven. Add in onions and garlic and sauté until fragrant, about 2 minutes. Add in diced tomatoes, tomato sauce, chilies, quinoa, chili powder, cumin, paprika, and about 1 1/2 cups of water. Season with salt and pepper as desired.

Bring to a low boil, then reduce heat to low. Cover and cook for about 30 minutes. Stir in beans, corn, cilantro and lime juice. Heat for another 5 minutes, then serve immediately.

Makes 6 servings; each serving 1 ½ cups.

NUTRITIONAL VALUE

1 serving: 275 Calories, 4g Fats, 29g Carbohydrates, 4.5g Fiber, 10g Protein, 5g Sugars.

SmartPoints Value:8

Mint Lemonade Slushy

Enjoy this delicious, thirst quenching drink on a hot, sultry day and feel your body tingle.

INGREDIENTS

3 1/2 cups ice

1 cup fresh spearmint leaves

1 1/2 cups water

1 cup lemon juice, freshly squeezed

Stevia to taste (I used about 1 tsp)

DIRECTIONS

Pulse all ingredients in blender until slushy-like texture is reached. Serve chilled in a frosted glass.

Makes 4 servings.

NUTRITIONAL VALUE

1 serving: 22 Calories, 2.5g Carbohydrates, 1g Fiber, 1g Sugar, 1g protein.

SmartPoints Value:0

Chapter 8: Weight Watchers at Christmas

Just because you are on a Weight Watchers program does not mean you cannot enjoy the holiday festivities with your family and friends. I have put together a few festive recipes which you can try. You might even consider making party-sized portions for your guests, as they may like to try something new and you won't even have to tell them they're eating smart!

Crockpot Lemon Rosemary Whole Chicken

INGREDIENTS

1 whole roasting chicken (about 6-8 lbs), cleaned and giblets removed

2 lemons, sliced

1 large onion, cut into wedges

3 sprigs fresh rosemary

2 tsp ground sage

1 tsp garlic powder

2 tbsp light butter

Salt and pepper to taste

DIRECTIONS

Preheat oven broiler. Sprinkle the inside of the chicken cavity with salt and pepper. Then place half of the lemons slices, half of the onion wedges and 2 sprigs of the rosemary inside. Place chicken inside a small roasting pan. Spread butter evenly all over the chicken, then season the chicken with the sage, garlic powder and salt and pepper.

Place chicken in oven and broil for about 8-10 minutes, just until the skin turns golden brown. If you like your chicken really darkened on the outside, leave it in until desired level of darkness is achieved. **To crisp the skin, you can do this step AFTER the slow cooking, if preferred.

Place remaining onions and a few of the remaining lemon slices in the bottom of the slow cooker. Now place the whole chicken on top. Top the chicken with remaining lemon slices, and rosemary leaves (removed from sprig). Cover with lid and cook on low for 6 – 8 hours or high for 4 – 5 hours.

Makes 4 servings.

NUTRITIONAL VALUE

1 serving: 300 Calories, 8g Fats, 30g Proteins, 9.5g Sugars

SmartPoints Value:8

Crusted Butternut Squash

INGREDIENTS

1 large butternut squash

1/3 cup whole wheat breadcrumbs

1/4 cup grated parmesan cheese

1 tsp dried sage

1 tsp garlic powder

1 tsp dried thyme

1 tsp dried parsley

Salt and pepper to taste

DIRECTIONS

Preheat oven to 400 degreesFahrenheit.

Line a large rimmed baking sheet with parchment paper and mist with cooking spray. Peel squash with a vegetable peeler. Cut in half lengthwise then scoop out all the seeds. Slice into 1/4" slices.

Place squash slices evenly in a single layer on the baking sheet. Mist generously with an olive oil mister.

In a small bowl, combine remaining ingredients. Sprinkle the breadcrumb mixture all over the top of the squash. Then mist lightly with the olive oil mister. Place in oven and bake until squash is tender and breadcrumb topping is golden brown, about 20-25 minutes.

Makes 4 servings.

NUTRITIONAL VALUE

1 serving: 119 Calories, 3g Fats, 21.5g Carbohydrates, 5g Protein, 3g Fiber.

SmartPoints Value:3

Cabernet Beef Pot Roast

INGREDIENTS

2 lbs pot roast

1 1/2 cups red wine, preferably Cabernet

2 tbsp light butter

5 garlic cloves, chopped

1 tsp dried thyme

1 tsp mustard seed

Salt and pepper to taste

DIRECTIONS

Preheat oven to 325 degreesFahrenheit and spray a small roasting pan with cooking spray or an olive oil mister.

Melt butter in a medium, nonstick skillet set over medium high heat. Season roast on all sides with salt and pepper. Place roast in skillet and brown evenly on all sides. Remove from pan and place into prepared roasting pan and set aside.

In the same pan that was used for browning the meat, add garlic and sauté until fragrant, about 1 minute. Add in wine, mustard seed, and thyme and stir, making sure to scrape up the browned bits on the bottom of the pan. Bring to a simmer, then remove from heat and pour over roast.

Cover roasting pan with aluminum foil. Place roast in oven, and cook for about 1 hour, or until internal temperature reaches 145 degrees. Let rest 10 minutes before slicing. Cut into 6 even slices and serve.

Makes 6 servings.

NUTRITIONAL VALUE

1 serving: 201 Calories, 6g Fats, 1.5g Carbohydrates, 29g Protein

SmartPoints Value:4

Turkey Sausage Patties

INGREDIENTS

1lb extra lean ground turkey (I used the kind from Jennie-O)

1 tbsp olive oil

1 tsp smoked salt

1 tsp pepper

1 tbsp brown sugar

1 tsp fennel seeds

1 tsp sage

1 tsp onion powder

1 tsp garlic powder

Pinch of allspice

DIRECTIONS

Day 1: Mix together all the spices in a small bowl. Then place the turkey in a medium sized bowl, add in the spices, and combine all ingredients using hands. Cover and refrigerate overnight.

Day 2: Spray a nonstick skillet with cooking spray or an olive oil mister, and set over medium heat. Form ground turkey into 8 patties, and place in pan. Cook until meat is no longer pink and is browned evenly on both sides. About 2-3 minutes per side. You can also use a lid to cover the pan while they are cooking to help them cook through the center better, and to help keep moisture in the meat, as extra lean turkey can be pretty dry.

Makes 8 servings.

NUTRITIONAL VALUE

1 serving; 79 Calories, 2.5g Fats, 1g Carbohydrates, 13g Protein.

SmartPoints Value:2

<u>Weight Watchers Raspberry Champagne Cocktail</u>

INGREDIENTS

¾ cup raspberry-cranberry juice, chilled

1-1/2 cups sparkling wine, chilled

1 cup lemon-lime seltzer, chilled

Ice cubes

½ cup fresh raspberries

4 small mint sprigs

DIRECTIONS

Combine the juice, wine and seltzer in a pitcher.
Fill 4 wine glasses with ice.
Divide the cocktail mixture evenly among the glasses. Garnish each glass with raspberries and a mint sprig.
Makes 4 servings.

NUTRITIONAL VALUE

1 serving: 99 Calories, 10g Carbohydrates, 1g Fiber

SmartPoints Value:3

Healthy Chocolate Coconut Truffles

INGREDIENTS

⅔ cup avocado, whipped (about 1 large)

¼ cup + 2 tablespoons unsweetened cocoa powder

½ teaspoon pure vanilla extract

1 teaspoon almond extract

⅔ cup milk chocolate chips

½ cup sweetened coconut flakes

DIRECTIONS

Blend the avocado in a food processor until smooth and creamy. Add in cocoa powder, vanilla and almond extract and continue processing until thoroughly combined.

In a medium microwave-safe bowl, heat chocolate chips in 30 second increments until melted. Stir well to ensure all chips are melted and chocolate is smooth.

Stir avocado mixture into the melted chocolate until well mixed. Cover bowl with plastic wrap and refrigerate for at least 2 hours. When you're ready to roll truffles, add sweetened coconut flakes to a shallow bowl.

Roll a rounded teaspoon of chocolate mixture into a small ball and roll in coconut to coat evenly.

Store chocolate truffles in refrigerator until ready to serve.

NUTRITIONAL VALUE

1 truffle per serving: 43 Calories, 3g Fats, 5g Carbs, 0.6g Fiber, 3.78g Sugar, 0.4g Protein

SmartPoints Value: 2

Low Fat Cranberry Bars

INGREDIENTS

2 eggs

¾ cup sugar

1 cup all-purpose flour

⅓ cup butter, melted

1 teaspoon vanilla

1-1/4 cups fresh or frozen cranberries

½ cup chopped walnuts

DIRECTIONS

Preheat oven to 350 degrees Fahrenheit.

Coat an 8-inch square baking pan with nonstick spray and set it aside.

In medium sized bowl beat the eggs until thick, about 5 minutes. Add the sugar and beat until creamy and well blended. Stir in the flour, butter and vanilla just until blended.

Stir in the cranberries and walnuts.

Scrape the batter into the prepared pan and spread it out evenly. Bake until set and a toothpick inserted in the center comes out clean, 40 to 50 minutes. Remove from the oven and place on a wire rack to cool completely. Cut into 16 bars.

Makes 16 servings.

NUTRITIONAL VALUE

1 serving: 122 Calories, 7g Fats, 19g Carbohydrates, 1g Fiber, 2g Protein

SmartPoints Value: 3

Weight Watchers Chocolate Mint Bars

INGREDIENTS

1 can (14 to 15 ounces) black beans, rinsed and drained

½ cup sugar

¼ cup unsweetened cocoa powder

¼ cup butter, melted

3 large eggs

½ teaspoon salt

½ teaspoon baking powder

¼ teaspoon vanilla extract

¼ teaspoon mint extract

2 tablespoons all-purpose flour

½ cup mini semisweet chocolate chips

3 tablespoons white chocolate chips

1 teaspoon vegetable oil

4 crushed peppermint candies

DIRECTIONS

Preheat oven to 350 degreesFahrenheit. Line an 8-inch square baking pan with nonstick aluminum foil.

Place the beans, sugar, cocoa powder, butter, eggs, salt, baking powder, vanilla and mint extract in the bowl of a food processor. Process on high until the mixture is completely smooth, scraping down the sides of the bowl several times.

Add the flour and semisweet chocolate chips. Pulse a few times until just blended.

Scrape the batter into the prepared baking pan. Spread out evenly. Bake until a toothpick inserted in the center comes out clean, 25 to 30 minutes. Remove from the oven and set on a wire rack to cool completely.

When the mixture is completely cool, make the topping.

Combine the white chocolate chips and oil in a small bowl. Microwave on high, stopping to stir every 20 to 30 seconds, until the chips are melted. Drizzle the melted white chocolate over the top of the cooled bars. Sprinkle with the crushed mints. Let cool and harden completely. Using the foil as handles, remove the whole slab of bars from the pan. Cut into 16 squares. Cut each square in half diagonally to make 32 triangles.

Makes 32 servings.

NUTRITIONAL VALUE

1 serving: 70 Calories, 3g Fats, 9g Carbohydrates, 1g Fiber, 2g Protein.

SmartPoints Value: 3

Tis the season to be jolly and just because you are on the Weight Watchers healthy lifestyle plan does not mean you cannot enjoy the festivities. Weight Watchers meals are visually attractive, smell aromatic and are mouth wateringly tasty. You would never believe they are good for you and your weight loss as well.

So pull out the tinsel, deck the halls and pull those crackers…Christmas is here!

Perhaps leave a treat for Jolly Saint Nick instead of the usual sugary snack. Mrs. Clause will thank you for it. And what's even better, with all the fresh veggies around you will have lots of snacks for Rudolph and his gang.

Chapter 9: Weight Watchers and Exercise

The Weight Watchers program focuses on the nutritional side of weight loss more so than the physical. Obviously all weight loss is increased with exercise. This is not to say you won't lose weight unless you exercise on Weight Watchers. Weight Watchers is just that – weight watching by eating correctly. Once you train your mind and body to accept healthy eating choices and you begin to lose weight, you will gain more confidence. Your energy levels will increase and many people go on and choose to do some form of exercise to burn off the new found energy and enthusiasm.

To lose weight you either have to reduce your intake of calories or burn off more calories than you take in daily. Imagine if you did both? Decrease intake and increase calories burnt. The weight would come off so much faster. This routine has to be exactly that – a routine. You cannot do it one day and then leave it for two weeks and do it again. It must be constant. Your mind and body need to be trained physically, as does your mind and body need to be trained to make healthy eating choices.

Exercise doesn't have to be something you dread every day. Choose something you enjoy doing and that doesn't become a task. Join a walking club of ladies. Laugh and chat along the way, make new friends and enjoy the scenery. During those hot summer months you could take up water aerobics or something else that is water related, depending on your fitness levels.

Basically any activity where you keep moving will aid your health and assist weight loss, you don't necessarily have to "work out" in a gym.

Our modern lives have made us "lazy." Cars, buses, elevators, escalators. Why catch the elevator for one floor? Stroll up the stairs instead. As you become fit, add a floor to your walk each day. You will feel yourself doing it quicker and easier. Soon you will be jogging up those stairs two by two.

There are many things we can do during our busy day to burn off calories.

Take a walk in the park at lunch time. Walk to the next office to see a colleague instead of just picking up the phone. Stand whenever possible instead of sitting down. Take time every so often to move around the office. All it takes is 30 minutes of energy burning movement every day to start your road to fitness.

At home, hide the TV remote and get up to change the channel. Wash your own car, and you won't believe how many calories you burn off doing just that. Walk your dog around the block. Stroll along while your children ride their bicycles; exercise for them and for you. Make it a family plan to be more active and get outside by planning a nightly walk or bike ride around the neighborhood before or after dinner. Getting your entire family involved will help you keep you motivated as you begin to change your lifestyle for the better.

Walk to the corner cafe for your milk and bread instead of taking the car.

As you start to feel better you will find your "exercise" period get longer.

Remember you are on Weight Watchers to better your health in the long run. This paired with daily exercise are health boosters all round.

You will start to feel GREAT. Exercise increases your metabolism which increases weight loss. Don't forget to tone your muscles. As you lose weight you will have to tone up because you might start to see extra sagging where your weight is falling off. Daily muscle toning can lower cholesterol and blood pressure, and reduces risks of strokes and heart attacks.

Your sleep patterns and quality of sleep will improve. Chemicals released during exercise also help to fight off depression. Exercise increases strength and flexibility. Your bones become healthier and stronger due to good eating patterns and exercise. And most importantly it will help you to maintain your goal weight for a lifetime.

If perhaps you are a "gym bunny" there are exercises you could concentrate on to help with your weight loss and body toning. Aerobic exercise that gets the heart rate up is excellent for weight loss and for fitness. Resistance training will help to tone up your body as you lose weight.

If you're serious about healthy eating and a healthy lifestyle then exercise is the next step.

Chapter 10: Tips for Increasing Water Consumption EveryDay

The rule should be to drink eight cups of water per day. Water is very important to our overall health and well being. Water flushes toxins from our bodies and aids our digestive system in staying regular. Drinking water prevents dehydration. Water assists with weight loss. Hydration of the skin reduces the signs of aging. Your body definitely feels healthier when it receives the right amount of water. Set goals for yourself to make sure you drink water throughout the day.

Don't drink any soda until you have had at leasttwo glasses of water.

Pick four points of your day (the same points for every day) where you drink a large glass of water - on waking up, on arriving at work, lunch time, and before you leave work for instance.

Carry an insulated water bottle which is full at all times.

Add fresh fruit to your water to give it flavor.

Add fizz to your water to change it up.

Snack on crushed ice or cubes throughout the day.

For every 10g grams of fat you eat, drink 20 ounces of water.

Water is an imperative part of daily health and effective weight loss.

Reach for that water and feel the health creep through your body.

Chapter 11: Cheat Days? Yes or No

There are varying opinions on the benefits of cheat days in a lifestyle plan such as Weight Watchers. There are times when you will want to have a day off and that is all good and well as you are only human. The entire point of a weight loss plan is to do just that - lose weight. It takes willpower, determination and most of all the need and wants to be lighter.

Don't get into the habit of cheat days early on. You tend to lose weight quicker earlier on as you have more weight to lose, so even with a cheat day you may still show lower digits on the scale. If you make a habit of this in the beginning it will be hard to stop. As the weight to lose becomes less, the cheat days may start to affect your weight loss. This is the time when people lose hope and give up. You get to that plateau stage and the scale won't move. Stick it out, be strong and refrain from cheat days until you have lost a good percentage of your overall weight loss goal.

You need these losses each week to boost your morale and keep you going. Dropping digits will keep you "hungry" for weight loss and your goal.

Set the goal you want to reach in stages. Perhaps weekly stages and promise yourself that when you have achieved week two, that you will allow yourself a treat just once in that month. Obviously, if this has negative effects on your weight loss you need to reconsider to once every two months or so. Everybody does deserve a treat now and then and a day to let your hair down. How, when and how often depends entirely on each person, their habits, hormones and own personal weight loss and gain history.

Keep in mind that treating yourself doesn't always have to involve food. Make a night for yourself to stay at home, let the kids go to a friend's house and read your favorite book or catch up on television shows you haven't watched in a while. Take yourself out for a manicure and/or pedicure, which will also help boost your confidence in your newly transforming body.

If at any time you have questions or need help or just some encouragement to get you through a rough patch, speak to the leader of your group. That is what they are there for. The other members are also there to lean on. You are all there for the same reason and you all, at some stage, have to fight off the same demons. Use each other as pillars of strength. More than likely there is someone else battling the same thing and is too afraid or embarrassed to speak up. SPEAK UP! If you don't, nobody knows you need helpand they can guide you or put you back on track.

Chapter 12: Who Can Do Weight Watchers

Weight Watchers is designed for people who need to lose weight. For someone who has a pre-existing medical condition, you should visit your local doctor first and inform him/her of your plans to join Weight Watchers. Allow the doctor to give you a thorough check up and discuss with you whether it is a good idea. Please do listen to whatever advice is given to you by the doctor.

Children may not join Weight Watchers. Children's bodies are still developing and changing at this stage and still need a variety of food sources to nurture growth and encourage brain development. If by the time a child is 17 and they have a problem with weight, they too can visit their local doctor for advice. People of 17 may join but they HAVE to have a letter of confirmation from their doctor.

Weight Watchers is not for pregnant women. The program is designed to help you lose weight and this is not something you want to be doing while pregnant. While pregnant you are feeding a whole extra person. You need to ensure you take in enough food and vitamins to keep yourself healthy and to encourage growth in your unborn child. By all means, join your local Weight Watchers group after the birth of your bundle of joy to encourage weight loss.

Chapter 13: Success Stories

When following a diet plan, it is difficult to see the light at the end of the tunnel, especially if you haven't seen anyone with results. What is wonderful about Weight Watchers is not only is this "diet" a way of life, making it easy to stay on track, but it is also full of community members with successful results and inspiring stories. On days where you feel that you simply can't continue with the diet plan, reading success stories can help reignite your drive towards a healthier lifestyle. The following success stories were taken directly from the Weight Watchers website, check out the website for additional information on the stories or even more success stories.

Use these success stories to serve as encouragement when feeling run down and hopeless; seeing others succeed while you feel you are failing can help you significantly. Reading about these individuals and listening to their words as they explain the hardships and exciting parts of their weight loss journey are priceless. No amount of money in the world can replace the feelings expressed through the words and statements these individuals recount.

GLORIA

Our first success story is Gloria. Gloria started her Weight Watchers journey at the age of 63, feeling helpless and unable to exercise due to her arthritis, she originally started with Weight

Watchers as a way to keep in touch with her family members. Here is a short excerpt in Gloria's words about her experience,

"Because I was 63 years old when I subscribed, I'd sort of given up on ever being slim again. My niece and daughters were going to start Weight Watchers Online on January 1, as a New Year's resolution and they asked if I'd do it with them. I thought, "What a great way to keep in touch!" I live in Minnesota, and my niece and daughters live in California and Iceland. We made a deal that we'd check in with each other at least once a week and share encouragement and recipes.

Before I started Weight Watchers Online, I ate too much. Both of my parents, two of my siblings, and two of my children are diabetic, so I've always been aware of following diabetic-friendly diets. But what I noticed shortly after subscribing was the astonishing amount of food I was actually eating. Cutting down on my portion sizes was my biggest challenge."

Gloria has a few tips for anyone else who intends to join the weight watchers journey:

Make olive oil spray your new best friend. I found I didn't use nearly as much oil as I previously used when I was measuring it out by hand.

Swap clothing! My daughters and I actually shared clothes back and forth as we got to different sizes. It was fun getting a free wardrobe re-vamp!

If you have a garage freezer, keep your frozen treats in there. Making the special trip will keep you mindful of what you're eating.

Share your success with others. I recently inspired a friend to join Weight Watchers Online. It made me so happy to know that I was helping others to get healthy as well.

Split entrées. In this country, our portion sizes are way too big! I found I was satisfied with half an entrée at most restaurants. The food was just as good, and I found I didn't have to stuff myself to feel satisfied.

DANIEL

A lot of men aren't aware that Weight Watchers works just as easily for men as it does for women. At the age of 41, Daniel weighed 235 pounds at the height of 5'11. After losing 60 pounds, Daniel feels as though he has a new lease on life and a greater sense of self. A short excerpt taken from Daniels own words on the Weight Watchers website is as follows,

"My wake-up call was when I sat down on my couch one morning to watch TV and I realized I couldn't see my waistband. It was completely covered by my belly. The light bulb just went on. I needed a change. I saw a Weight Watchers for Men commercial on ESPN and thought that following the Plan online would be a good fit for me.

I knew I needed structure, but I didn't want to exclude anything from my diet. Other diets make you count calories or carbs, but Weight Watchers just gives your daily PointsPlus Target. This food equals this PointsPlus value. Done. It's also easy to use on the go which I needed because I travel a lot. Weight Watchers Online is great with helping someone like me who didn't want to go to meetings. I wanted to do it on my own, and Weight Watchers gave me the tools I needed to do just that. I read the instructions and over time learned more and more about the Plan.

The app with the eTools that I use on my smartphone is the best invention ever. I use the mobile site and also the Food Tracker and the Barcode Scanner app during grocery shopping. I also love that restaurants like Applebee's have menu items in the food database right on my phone. Then I can track right there in the restaurant and know how many PointsPlus values I have left for the day.

Why wait to get started? There's no reason to wait. I put it off and put it off, and I regret it. I'm in the best shape of my life, and I look the best I've ever looked. Once you start, you get out exactly what you put in. If you cheat, you're only cheating yourself. A lot of guys have this mindset that you only eat salads while dieting. But with Weight Watchers, you don't have to give anything up. Every person is different. For me, it's no fried foods or soda. But I still get my steak and pizza when I want it. If you're a huge soda fan you can have it — just cut other things out. You can make this Plan your own based on your individual tastes."

KERRY

Another inspiring success story is Kerry. After being diagnosed with Crohn's Disease and anemia, Kerry was too exhausted to play with her kids, let alone even think about starting a diet plan. She explained that her wake-up call was when she went on vacation with her family and realized how bogged down she was with health ailments and pain, completely unable to enjoy herself. After coming home from the vacation, she signed up for Weight Watchers, and she made a pact with herself to lose 52 pounds in 52 weeks, completing her goal even earlier than she thought.

Taken directly from the Weight Watchers website is a short excerpt in Kerry's words about her Weight Watchers journey.

"I was concerned at first about being able to find healthy food options in spite of my Crohn's Disease. But surprisingly I didn't have any trouble with the extra fiber or increased fruits and veggies. The biggest challenge was getting enough protein since I don't eat red meat, nuts, or pork. So I choose things like chicken and fish. I also pick things like Greek yogurt over regular yogurt since it has more protein. I wanted to take this year for myself primarily so my health would get better. I didn't know if my Crohn's would get better or not and I was really at high risk for developing diabetes.

Both of my parents have diabetes, and I knew with my weight I was really close to following suit. Now my energy level is so much higher. I've been able to go off my blood pressure medicine and my acid reflux medicine, which is saving me about a thousand dollars a year. That's just remarkable! My family doctor asked if I would write a letter to the local newspaper sharing my story because everyone comes into his office asking for more medication or a pill to lose weight. He said it was amazing for someone to come in and be off these medications after a year. It's been such a reward to know that my health is in a better place than it ever was before.

I'd said I wanted to lose 52 pounds in 52 weeks, and I actually reached my goal much earlier. I got to 52 pounds in about eight months. And on my one-year anniversary, I was still down 54 pounds. It was a combination of emotions. I was just amazed that I had done it. I had razor sharp focus this year. Reaching goal was such a powerful moment to realize that I set a goal, I was able to do it, and I've been able to maintain it and stay on Plan."

JOY

After years of being overweight, Joy's wake-up call was when her daughter who requires special needs, slipped away from her, running towards the street. Due to her size, she was unable to catch her daughter when she got away. Appalled at seeming inability to properly care for her child, she decided to begin attending Weight Watchers meetings with her coworkers. Joy felt as though she was a bad mother because she was unable to stop her child from darting towards a busy street and this was the push she needed to take her weight and her health into her own hands. Taken directly from the Weight Watchers website, Joy states in her words the journey of gaining back her sense of self and becoming a better mother for her child.

"I'd been overweight for most of my life and had accepted that that was just who I was. I blamed genetics and my Italian heritage for my appearance. We all love to cook, bake, host parties, entertain and eat! My parents were both obese and died young – my mother from diabetes, my father from a heart attack. I never used to think of myself as being able to get old, probably because I never got to see my grandparents as old people. But Weight Watchers has given me the gift of vision. I can now imagine myself one day as a thin active grandparent running around with my grandkids.

I originally set a goal for myself to walk three to four times a week and to participate in at least one 5K per week as a walker. I later began to incorporate some running. With encouragement from my husband and friends, I am proud to say I've now completed my first 10K mud run and my first half marathon at Disney World!"

Joy also has a few tips for anyone beginning their weight loss journey, sharing her keys and tips to a successful journey. Joy states that once you have a setback, which we all do, aim to meet one of your Good Health Guidelines to make up for it. Meeting one of the guidelines will give you a positive focus as opposed to focusing on the negatives and things you didn't achieve for the day. Joy quoted her leader who says, "It's not how hard you fall, but how high you bounce."

Joy also stated she takes advantage of the recipes builder. She talks about how much fun it is to find new recipes and plug in substitutions and watching the PointsPlus values go down. Joy also recommends fitting in the meetings whenever or wherever you can. Making it to the meetings can be the difference between succeeding by having a healthy support system or falling flat on your face. At the end of her journey, Joy lost close to 100 pounds.

BRUCE

Bruce is an example of someone who lost weight with another person, his wife. Sometimes, having someone beside you to push and pull you into shape is the drive you need to make life changes. Bruce didn't think he needed to lost weight. However, his wife thought differently. Sometimes, looking at yourself every day in the mirror can cause us to get used to what we see and not pay attention to the weight we are gaining in different areas and the effect that it is having on our health. Bruce is an excellent example of this.

Weight watchers interviewed Bruce about how he was able to change his eating habits and work with his wife to create a new way of thinking, cooking and eating. Weight watchers asked: What drove your decision to lose weight? Bruce stated "My wife and I travel a lot. When we returned from a cruise in the beginning of 2011, she suggested that we both lose 10 pounds before our planned biking trip in the Italian Alps. I told her I didn't need to lose weight. Knowing I really did, she dragged me kicking and screaming to my first Weight Watcher's meeting. I am glad she did.

It was a very good process. The program changes your thinking. We always ate healthily, but we ate too much. We always exercised, but not enough. Following the program, I lost 31 pounds in about five months. I love that I now wear a size-32 pants. My wife also hit her goal. We're both lifetime members."

When asked by Weight Watcher's, "How easy was this Plan to pick up and sustain?" to which Bruce answered, "It was mostly a cinch. The biggest change was portion control. Tracking and weighing food helped me with that. We still go to meetings every week. I find them to be very important. They reinforce everything you've learned. I weigh in every week, even though as a lifetime member you don't have to. If I weighed in just once a month, I'd be worried about getting off track. Now, if I gain one week, I know then and can adjust to where I need to be at the following week."

MAE

Approaching the big 3-0 at close to 300 pounds, Mae was embarrassed with herself and her diet choices. Unable to climb two flights of stairs without becoming winded, Mae knew she needed to make a huge change in her life to avoid the looming health affects her weight was beginning to have on her. After jumping into the online Weight Watcher's program, Mae has lost close to 130 pounds of her old self, revealing a confident, empowered woman beneath it all. In Mae's words on the Weight Watchers website, Mae states:

"When you're overweight all your life, it's always in the back of your head. I would constantly say, "I'll start Monday," or "The first day of the month is coming up. I'll start then." It would always be another excuse. I'd tried other diets in the past and had actually lost about 70 pounds on a low-carb plan. The problem with that was that I wanted a doughnut every single day of my life. So when I finally broke down, I would have ten doughnuts instead of one. I gained all the weight back and then some. Being over 280 pounds, I was on the fast track to Type II diabetes, high blood pressure, and cholesterol, you name it. My 30th birthday was coming up, and I finally decided once and for all to get healthy. Weight Watchers appealed to me because it's not really a diet. It's more like healthy guidelines for lifelong eating habits. I subscribed to Weight Watchers online and hadn't looked back.

At my heaviest, I wanted to blend into the background as much as possible. I didn't want anyone to notice me. I wouldn't wear makeup and would just throw my hair into a sloppy bun. But now before I go to sleep I'm thinking about what I'll wear to work the next day and how I'll do my hair. It's just strange because I've never been a girly girl, and now I care about shoes and how a certain necklace looks with a certain dress. I walk around like I own the place sometimes, and I love it. Weight Watchers taught me that this was how life should be for everyone, not just those trying to lose weight. I am so much healthier now. I'm not quite at my goal weight yet, but I constantly have my eye on the prize. Other than losing weight, there are other successes as well. Now I have a slightly out-of-control shopping habit since I can buy single-digit sizes now."

DENEENE

Another success story is a woman named Deneene. Deneene began eating due to the stress of having a miscarriage. While pregnant with her second child, staying healthy was her number one goal. Although she tried to remain healthy, she noticed it was becoming more and more difficult to exercise and stay healthy. From the Weight Watchers website, Deneene states

"While I was on maternity leave a friend of mine told me about the success she was having with Weight Watchers at Work meetings. Since I knew

I wouldn't have the time to attend meetings with a newborn, I decided to sign up for Weight Watchers Online. I didn't tell anyone about it at the beginning in case I didn't end up losing the weight. But I set small goals and have lost 23 pounds. * When I went back to work I was able to track my progress online and also plan out my meals. Now I tell everyone that I use Weight Watchers Online and how easy it is. People tell me they can't believe I just had a baby, and that makes me feel great.

I love the energy that I have now. I can sit on the floor with my daughter and get up without the effort it used to take. I'm also finally able to wear some of my old clothes again. It's been so long since I've worn some of them that it feels like I'm shopping every time I go into my closet!"

Although only a few stories are listed, there are millions of people who have lost weight using the Weight Watchers diet program. Many will speak of the importance motivation, support, and organization when it comes to losing weight, but many other aspects come into play as well. Some people need a health scare to motivate them, some people are unable to motivate themselves without the motivation of a friend alongside them throughout the journey, others may be able to look at a photograph and motivate themselves that way. We all have different motivators, be it health, kids, work, lifestyle, energy – find what motivates you and use it to create your success story.

Chapter 14: Tips For Success From The Successful

Though many of us are successful in the weight loss journey, there is no set in stone technique for all of us to be successful all of the time. What makes us each unique and different also makes it difficult to find an all-encompassing, weight loss plan that works for everyone. What is fantastic about the Weight Watcher's community and success stories is that everyone has different tips and tricks that helped them get ahead and stay ahead. You don't need to be an expert to know what works for you and what doesn't and sharing these tips with other individuals could help other people just as easily as it helped you. These tips are shared below and are direct quotes from real Weight Watcher's success stories.

The following three tips are from Danielle, age 36 who lost 48 lbs.

"I switched from chips to grapes for a snack, as I tend to mindlessly eat. That doesn't mean to eat 10 watermelons because they're free, but you can still snack without worry."

"Just because you go out, doesn't mean you can't stay on plan. In my clutch, I keep my lipstick, phone, and my Tracker."

"Confidence is the best accessory you can ever ask for. It goes with absolutely every outfit!"

The following tip is from Phee, age 60 who lost 61 lbs.

"I like to give advice to people my age, because even younger girls in their 40s will say, "Oh I'm getting too old to do that." No. There's no such thing. There's no such thing as being too old to lose weight. And to maintain the weight, that's a big deal too."

The following tip is from Sharonda, age 30 who lost 222.6 lbs.

"The meetings are amazing. It's like a community because there are people there from all walks of life, but we all have the same goal: to lose weight. You learn so much from the others who are going through the same struggles as you. If you have an unexpected gain, everyone is there to help. My Leader, Jamie, has been one of my biggest supporters."

The following tips are from Katie, age 33 who lost 85 lbs.

"For lunch, I used to go out or eat in the cafeteria. Now, I bring lunch every day. I ask myself, how many PointsPlus® values do I want to use? I plan. Budgeting is key. I haven't felt deprived a single day."

"I think you have to go slow and not get too overwhelmed. Mini goals are really important. Don't try to do everything all at once. I did everything slowly: learned how to use eTools, listened to people at meetings, started to exercise and read Message Boards in the WeightWatchers.com Community. I found that the tools I needed were inside me all along. Weight Watchers just helped unlock them."

"I think my biggest change was going from a mindless eater to a mindful eater. Weight Watchers taught me that you could enjoy food without sacrifice. I was always either on a diet or off, and thought of my eating as "good" or "bad." Now I've taken those words out of my vocabulary. My good habits have even benefited my husband, who lost weight just by eating the food I'm cooking. And I've lost 86 pounds*!"

The following tips are from Joseph, age 33 who lost 88 lbs.

"My wife and I love cooking together now! Using recipes from Weight Watchers.com allows us to still eat the foods we love, but in lightened-up ways."

"My wife and I also love the outdoors so we'll go for two-hour walks. It's a great feeling to not be winded and exhausted at the end of it."

The following tip is from Clarence, age 29 who lost 50 lbs.

"Stop lying to yourself. You packed on the pounds. You know something needs to be done. It's time to address it. You need a sustainable program – a life change. There's nothing you can't eat. You can even eat pizzas and go to buffets. This plan works."

The following tips are from Ester, age 57 who lost 25 lbs.

"Keep going to the meetings. My leader always answers any questions I have about the plan and motivates us to continue to stay on track and do our best."

"Walk, run, dance, whatever you like, but move, move, move! I'm a huge dessert person. I love ice cream. So if I want ice cream at the end of the day, I know I have to get my 10,000 steps in."

"Have patience. Think of how long it took you to gain the weight. It's going to come off just as gradually. Stick with it and you'll see the results."

"Stick with it and persevere. It's a struggle at times, but the end result is worth it."

Chapter 15: Interesting Facts about Weight Watchers

- ✓ Weight Watchers was founded by Jean Nidetch. She started the program after a neighbor thought she was pregnant.

- ✓ The First meeting in the UK was held near Windsor in 1967 and since then there have been more than 6000 meetings.

- ✓ Weight Watchers has gained over 1 million members in their 52 years.

- ✓ Average weight loss after three months at Weight Watchers is 8.6lbs.

- ✓ Weight Watchers is NHS approved.

- ✓ In 2013, Weight Watchers posted profits of almost $24 million. It is a very profitable business.

- ✓ Sarah Ferguson claims Weight Watchers saved her life.

- ✓ In 2008, Kim from the USA claimed to have lost 211.8lbs in just two years on Weight Watchers.

- ✓ In 2010, the floor at a meeting in Sweden collapsed under the weight of 20 members busy with a meeting.

- ✓ It took up until 2011 for calorie counting to be dismissed as ineffective.

Conclusion

With the information and recipes contained in this book as your starting point, you are on the right track to maintaining your Weight Watchers SmartPoints budget. Making sure that you stay within your daily allowance, and that any overages are accounted for with your weekly allowance, will mean success in your attempt to lose weight and, more importantly, eat healthier.

Keep in mind that we all slip up occasionally, so don't beat yourself up about it as that will only make you more likely to continue slipping up. Use the success stories as inspiration when you get discouraged and utilize the resources in this book when heading to the grocery store and cooking for you and your family. With each recipe you try, you bring yourself closer to continuing a lifelong, healthy lifestyle.

Along with the recipes listed in this book, there is a wealth of other recipes throughout the internet and other books. Don't simply limit yourself to the recipes and tips in this book because there are thousands more out there for you to discover and try. Sticking with the same recipes over and over again could cause you to get bored and make you more likely to fall off the wagon.

Other ways to stay successful are by sharing this book with a friend and cooking together. You can each put your own spin on different recipes and give each other advice and encouragement while cooking. It is sometimes easier for people to enter the weight loss journey with a friend or family member as opposed to going at it alone. Support and encouragement can be all some people need. Weight Watcher's online not only offers support on the website, but also allows you to communicate with other individuals directly and attend different meetings in areas close to you whether you are at home, work, in a temporary location or on vacation.

Making goals for yourself is a good way to make sure you stay on track. For example, if you want to get better at cooking and making meals for yourself and your family, opt to try a new recipe every week; maybe even two recipes? This way, you can get the joy of trying new foods while also keeping yourself healthy and instilling new habits in your everyday routine. Another goal could be to walk 10,000 steps in a day. This a goal we should all strive for, but it can be difficult to achieve for some of us with such busy, sedentary schedules. Instead of sitting down all day, take regular interval breaks where you walk around the office. To start, make it a goal to walk 250 steps every two hours. You can get a pedometer from any store nearby to help track your steps – smartphones will even track your steps for you now, though they may not be entirely accurate. Shooting for a small goal like this can be the start of something huge and will have a large impact on the success of your weight loss and maintenance over time.

Meal preparation is a great way to get ahead of the week before it even starts. By cooking meals and preparing them at the end of the weekend, this gives you extra time throughout the week to exercise and allow time for other activities you may not have otherwise had time for. For example, make a batch of egg sandwiches and label them for each day, then each morning grab one on your way to work. You can do this for your lunches as well. Dinner can be a bit trickier if you have a family to cook for, but your mornings and lunches will be packed which will save you time at night that you don't have to spend preparing for the next day.

Different areas of your life can have different weaknesses – some people can't live without their iced coffee in the morning whereas other people simply wouldn't dream of going an entire day without a soda. It is possible to lose weight and enjoy these guilty pleasures but in moderation. With each setback or guilty pleasure, you indulge in, you have to make sure you are staying on track every day and keeping to your goal or you will be even more inclined the continuously loose track. Some people make goals to walk or exercise for a certain amount of time for each guilty pleasure they indulge in. For example, ten more minutes on the treadmill for half a can of Coca-Cola. This obviously varies per individual, but you get the basic idea.

Overall, one of the best ways to stay on track is through support and encouragement. It is nearly impossible to succeed when you are surrounded by people who aren't going through the same battle that you are. Because of this, it can be close to impossible for you to stay focused when you are constantly being tempted every which way for a myriad of different reasons, be it food, laziness, etc. Make sure you surround yourself with a great support group at home, work and in social circles. If nothing else, make sure you attend meetings to get the support you need if you aren't getting it at home or in the workplace. Talking and venting to the people and your coaches at the Weight Watchers meetings can help keep you on track when you feel like you aren't going to be able to make it much further. Offering words of encouragement and pushing you to persevere and remember why you are fighting this battle and why it is important to you is why your coaches and leaders are there. They want you to succeed, and they will make sure you do, all you have to do is ask and speak up.

Be sure to remind yourself of the importance of regular exercise in addition to your Weight Watchers plan. Adding in 30 minutes or more a day of exercise can assure you meet your goal of 1-2 pounds of weight loss a week. If you are unsure about how to begin your exercise regime, consult your local Weight Watcher's office or online community – even visit your local gym to get some free pointers and decide if you want to sign up. There are millions of different ways to exercise and no one way works for everyone so it is important to listen to your body and pay attention to what works and what doesn't. One of the greatest gifts you can give yourself is the gift of health with this book, you can either supplement your current health endeavor or use this book to kick start your journey.

I hope that you have found this book useful and that you enjoy the recipes provided within. I wish you great luck and success in your Weight Watchers endeavor.